Earthen Vessel

James Hay
Ordinary Man

by

Maureen Hay Read

International Standard Book Number: 1-883294-01-0
Library of Congress Number: 93-83125
Printed in the United States of America.

Library of Congress Cataloging-in-Publication Data

Read, Maureen Hay, 1937-
    Earthen Vessel, James Hay, Ordinary Man / Maureen Hay
Read
    188p.   cm.

    1. Hay, James—Biography.   2. Christian biography-
United States. I. Title.
                                        93-83125
                                        CIP

Published by
Olde Springfield Shoppe
10 West Main Street, P. O. Box 171
Elverson, PA 19520-0171

"We have this

treasure in

EARTHEN VESSELS

that the excellency

of the power

may be of God

and not of us."

II Corinthians 4:7

James Hay visiting Grand Canyon in 1992.

DEDICATION

To his grandchildren:

Melissa	Susan
Sylvia	Michael
James	Anne

and Elizabeth who lives in Another Place

Contents

IRISH DIALECT

Used In *Earthen Vessel*

weanes - wee ones or children
strand - shore or beach
lough - lake
byre - cow barn
whin bushes - bushes with brilliant yellow
    blooms in May and June
praties - potatoes
scaulding - scolding
jersey - pull-over sweater
co-op - the cooperative store in Creeslough in
    which people had a share
scone - bread
turf - peat dug from the hillsides and boglands
broughen - oatmeal
Cutye, Tutsie - pet names for girls
park - an area of land with mostly bushes,
    hedges, wasteland

Introduction

Biographical books are usually about those persons who have succeeded at business or sports, those who have done something sensational or unique, those who are famous, the so-called beautiful people. Thus, they are beyond the reach of most of us.

However, it is to ordinary folk that I address this book, men and women who live humdrum lives, earthen vessels, without glamor or excitement or even contentment, but who look for the Treasure which transforms lives and gives purpose to the drabbest life. This book is for you, an average person who longs for meaning in life.

The man in this book—James Hay—was born along with ten brothers and sisters on a tiny farm in windswept Donegal, Ireland. When he was nineteen, he came to the United States where he met and married a young American woman named Emily.

And here in this country, he also met the Savior, Christ the Lord, the object of a long quest. It was the beginning of life with joy and purpose and an amazing peace of mind. It was too good to keep to himself and his goal was to tell all whom he met of the Good News.

His friendship with God along the common road of life is chronicled here. The story is authentic, altogether true—of a simple earthen vessel, a factory worker filled with the gold of Christ. James is an ordinary man who lives an extraordinary life with God.

How do I know this? Because he is my Dad.

— **Maureen Hay Read**
P. O. Box 39, Narvon, PA 17555

It seemed to James, now that he was older, that those early years in Ireland were exceedingly good ones. Memories of hard work, chilblains, gnawing hunger, and chilly damp wind could not obliterate the warmth, the love, the remarkable stability that his boyhood had given him.

Now, six decades later, as he sat by the kitchen window at Narvon and prayed, his thoughts ran back, back to his boyhood, down past the byre, through the meadow to the lake with cloud-shadows upon it, then back into his mother's kitchen, that center of family strength and laughter and crowded living, with the mingled odors of raisin scone baking and wet shoes drying by the fire, then outside again with a glance at mist-covered Muckish and the sea shining in the distance...

Bless the Lord, O my soul...
and all that is within me,
bless His holy Name.
Bless the Lord, O my soul,
and forget not all His benefits.

Chapter 1

Donegal in the northwest corner of Ireland was a rich, energetic green in 1909 as it was every year. But in midsummer there was an increased lushness to the countryside, punctuated with the gold of ripening oats and the dark brown of rickled turf, with sun-struck whin bushes and heather gradually turning the hills to pink.

The days were long and luminous. It was the time of year when it scarcely got dark, a few hours, but even then there was a sense of expectancy of the dawn. The hens were hardly settled in til the rooster's first crow could be heard with male insistence that his womenfolk wake up when he did.

Anne used to wonder how hens managed to be so productive in the summer when they got so little sleep. She heard Maggie scooting the chickens outside again. Two careless ones had wandered into the kitchen as Anne was laboring in the tiny bedroom.

It shouldn't be so hard, she thought tiredly, when it's the eighth one. She was already the mother of four sons and three daughters. Having a baby was nearly as commonplace as digging potatoes, yet Anne moaned on her bed in a new agony. She was as alone in this as Eve with her firstborn, waiting for each pang, waiting for deliverance.

Maggie Moore, her neighbor, was there to help, she and Nurse Doyle. Maggie had a houseful of weanes herself whom Anne had helped deliver in turn.

1

"Go on ye, boys, outside! Ye've got turnips to thin," scolded Maggie through the door. Anne knew they were curious and worried. It was taking longer than it should.

"Where are the girls?" she asked Maggie.

"They're playing with wee George in the kitchen," said Maggie. "I gave them tea and some scone I baked. I knew ye'd na' be able to make bread the day."

The pain enveloped her again, shutting out all else. She was so hot and the door to this tiny room had to be shut. Was there no air?

"Open the window," she gasped.

"It is open," said Maggie. "Ye're nearly there, Anne."

There was another pain, then another and Anne could hardly get her breath. At last she heard Maggie's delighted cry.

"Ah, thanks be, he's here, a fine wee boy. Not so wee, Anne. He's a big boy. No wonder it took him a lang time to get here."

Nurse Doyle, quietly, deftly managed Anne, and Maggie took the new weane and bathed him.

Within minutes she had laid him beside Anne whose arm curved as naturally around him as a cat's tail around itself. She was so very tired, but it was all over, a hard day's work. She could sleep.

Another son. This one will be James, she thought drowsily, after John's father. James was a good solid name. It fit this extra-long baby who was already restless and squirming and searching for his dinner. John would be proud of another son when he came home on Saturday night.

Anne often wished John was at home especially when she bore her babies, but then they would have been much poorer. He had a job, something few men in Donegal had in those days, and she was grateful.

For it was indeed a most unpretentious home and neighborhood that James Hay was born into that July, 1909. The Hays lived in a small gray stone house built by John and his eldest son Willie, along the Rooskey Road just a mile or more from the village of Creeslough. The countryside was nearly treeless, rugged, inhospitable land, that yielded mostly rocks, heather, whin bushes, and peat bogs.

Around the homes on the Rooskey Road were tiny sloping farms, fertile enough, but too small to produce more than potatoes and a little grain for the cows and chickens that lived there. Beyond were magnificent hills over which sheep wandered. It was beautiful country, but hard for farmers to eke out a living. And in Donegal, what was there else to do besides farm?

Creeslough was a dozen or more houses, a post office, three pubs, a couple of shops, and two churches, one for each faith, Catholic and Protestant. Set on a small hill, the village overlooked the strand where the sea came in twice a day.

Anne loved the sea. Whenever she went to shop in Creeslough, she would stand briefly at the eastern edge of town and look out over the sea. Across the strand where the tide was moving, she could faintly see in the distance the village of Downings where she had lived as a girl.

Anne had grown up near the seashore at Downings, and the pull of the tides and the cycles of the moon she almost felt in her own body. Her brothers were hardy fishermen and farmers. Thus it had been given to her, growing up, the job of keeping the cows in the high hills of Ganye behind her home. There she had spent hours of her childhood alone watching the cows eat, looking out across the bay, enduring mist, wind, loneliness. Cows were poor company for one so vibrant and warm. Anne loved people, her own people.

Which was why, after she was married at nineteen, she often walked the ten miles back to Downings. She missed her family, the strong odor of her brothers' clothes after they had handled fish all night, the creak of the fish carts as they trundled along the road to the Creeslough station, the sound of the tide coming in, the friendly villagers. Rooskey, her new home, was a lonely place and John Hay, ten years her senior, a quiet man. When the cows were milked, the hens fed, her floor swept clean,

3

The Hay family at Rooskey, Creeslough in Donegal County, Ireland. Left to right: Rebecca, George, James (author's father), John and Anne (author's grandparents), Sandy, Thomas, and Mary Hay.

the fire banked, she would put on her coat and hat and walk, slowly at first, then more quickly as the miles became fewer, to her old home.

But as her babies came on every two years or so, Anne's roots dug in more deeply at Rooskey like the sturdy whin bushes on the north side of the house. She became far too busy and too tired to face that walk. When they moved from the small dark old house to this new one that John himself built, it became home to her.

Her kitchen was the heart of the home. In fact it might have been the only room as far as the children were concerned. Everything of importance happened there except actual sleeping, all the eating, drying one's feet, talking, playing, working, just plain living was done in that one friendly room. Its center was the fireplace in the north wall where a large black pot hung on the crane and a smoke-blackened teapot sat on the hob. In both summer and winter a turf fire burned steadily, drawing those around to sit near its warm coals. Sparely furnished, the room had only a sideboard, a large table, several chairs, and a bench in the corner next to the fire. The flagstone floor was uneven but scrubbed frequently to remove the effects of muddy shoes and frequent eating and drinking.

How Anne enjoyed the morning sun pouring in her east kitchen window warming the gray stone floor—unless it rained, an all too frequent event. On those days she would hurry to get the fire blazing and the kettle boiled. Sometimes she forgot to have some turf inside and it would sputter uncertainly for the first half hour, then settle into a steady, cozy heat.

Tea, what a comfort on a cold, bleak morning. Anne would sit on the bench in the corner next to the fire, drinking the tea, warming her hands around the cup, and on the hob thaw her feet which were chilled by the work in the byre.

This was her home, hers and John's. They had about eight acres of sloping (steeply at places), rocky, nearly treeless land, between the Rooskey Road and the lough at the bottom of the meadow, and two more acres on the other side of the road. On this small farm they raised potatoes, oats, turnips, whin bushes, heather, three cows, a couple pigs, and several dozen chickens.

Since John worked away from home, it fell on Anne to supervise the farm. She had to decide what to plant, when to harvest, whether or not to cut hay on a cloudy morning, how many eggs to sell and to keep, when to kill an old rooster that had outlived his usefulness—and then do it herself. She made butter each week, selling most of it along with the eggs, but kept enough to eat with the scones she baked regularly.

With her health and vitality, she handled farming, loneliness, a new baby every two years, and the absence of her husband, often when she sorely needed him.

John Hay was a good man, loyal, dependable, intelligent, but as silent and inscrutable as a spider when he sat quietly on a weekend with a book, reading busily page after page, spinning a web of aloofness and privacy around himself until Anne would impatiently brush it away with a sharp request to rock the baby or lift a crying weane.

A first-rate stone mason and an incredibly swift worker, he had no trouble getting jobs even in Ireland. Each Sunday afternoon he left home to work another week as a builder for the railroad.

He and Jimmy Dugan, who lived across the lough in Craig, would leave with one bicycle between them, John on the bike riding down the road, the other one walking. After a couple miles, he would leave the bike by the side of the road and go on walking while Jimmy came from behind, picked up the bicycle and rode another two miles past John. In this way they would reach their job, each one riding half way and walking the other half, up to twenty miles altogether.

At the end of the week on Saturday evening, they returned home the same way, sometimes stopping at the pub for a drink. Not often though. John liked to keep his head clear so he could study over the weekend.

6

A rear view of the Hay home in Ireland with a pile of turf (peat) to the left of the house.

Studying and reading were John's passion. But with his quickly enlarging family, there was simply no money for books or newspapers. No farmer could afford them in those days. Yet a man, driven as he was to know, to learn, had to find them somehow.

John's curious, inquiring mind led him to bookish friends, Master Durning, a teacher at a nearby school, and Andrew Wilkinson, a local businessman. With the generosity of these two, John was able to assuage somewhat his compelling thirst for knowledge by borrowing their books.

Anne had little patience with him and this chronic, insatiable need to learn. She had a keen enough mind herself, but when a weane was crying or a field of praties needed to be dug or a wife needed cheering, a man had no business going off looking for something to read. Sometimes she would set the cradle near his foot with a curt request to keep it in motion while he read. John would quietly comply. Anne's tongue could be sharp.

Yet John provided for his family better than most fathers did in those days because of his job away from home. Anne knew this. She also liked the feeling of being in charge of the home-place. John trusted her. She could sell a pig for a profit or thin the turnips as well as any man. When the babies were small, she would lay them on a blanket while she planted potatoes. They kicked and cooed, and if a bit of Irish mist dampened them, it seemed only to make their cheeks pinker. And a neighbor might come along and help a day or two. Somehow she was always able to manage.

Then as her sons grew older, they helped her. Willie, her oldest, was made to work nearly as soon as he could walk, yet like his father, he had a yearning to study. As the years went by, even though he missed school often to help at home, he managed to educate himself beyond the limits of the Crees-lough school. At thirteen, he was hired by the local railroad station, where he worked steadily til he left for Derry and a job at the Port.

With Robert, Anne's second son, it was different. He loathed school and feared his teacher. All too often he had been caned, and though he may have deserved a scaulding, it hurt Anne to think of a boy, a big boy, cringing under Miss Wilkinson's cane. Anne thought there were better ways to control a child than beating him regularly.

And so, Robert, as time went on, was the one who most often missed school to do the plowing and planting and harvesting, which then made it even more difficult when he went back. But how he enjoyed being at home, working hard all day, safe from the persecution of the tart Miss Wilkinson.

After Robert came Johnny, her third son, the one who looked most like her. Anne smiled whenever she remembered small Johnny wandering away one day from his brothers. His short legs grew weary, and he had curled up behind a rock to sleep. There a neighbor child had found him and rushed home. "Mammy, there's a fairy sleeping behind yon rock!"

"Haul' your tongue, weane, there's not. The fairies don't be seen now, only in the evenin' or the dawn."

"Mammy, there is, there is. Come and see."

The boy insisted, so she followed him and found Johnny sound asleep, then came laughing to tell Anne who had begun to wonder where the child was.

That was Johnny, smaller than the others, fine-boned, quietly nimble and good-natured, able to do a job with hardly anyone noticing him, rather like a leprechaun indeed. He was a great help to Anne, especially with the little sisters who came next, Margery, Annie Jane, and Mary, for he never got upset nor excited.

Anne was glad to have daughters. Every woman needed a girl and now she had three. It was time to stop.

But no, she was having sons again. There came George, born with a club foot, twisted, wrinkled, even smaller than the other foot. How had it happened? He must have lain within her the wrong way. A son who was crippled, what a cruel thing. How could he work? And if he couldn't work, of what use was he? How could he live?

But as the years went by, George turned out to be as tireless as the others, and perhaps one of the brightest. He was nearly as bookish as his father, yet like John, he worked swiftly and efficiently. Still she kept him in school as much as possible. Better to let Robert farm and George learn. That might make life a little easier for him later.

She was the mother of seven, a large enough family, but when the eighth came along, she had room for him. Little James joined the family quietly, without much notice, just part of a day's work. When John, his father, saw him for the first time the next weekend, he smiled and said, "Anne, he's a fine wee boy. Ye've done well." He touched her shoulder briefly.

That was all, but she knew he was pleased. The next she saw him, he was in the corner by the fire with a week-old newspaper. A neighbor came in and they were soon engrossed in making plans for a new building at the neighbor's farm. Given the measurements of a house or barn, John could calculate with precision how much stone and lumber were needed.

9

Anne held James tightly in her arms and nursed him. The largest of her babies, he was also the fussiest. Her milk, which had satisfied all the others, was not enough for him.

Yet hungry or not, it didn't stunt his growth. She clad him in a dress to confound the wee people, who were known to steal little boys. He soon outgrew his cradle and had to sleep in a bed with his brothers in the low attic upstairs. George was responsible to help him up and down the steps each night and morning though there were some tumbles aong the way.

Anne watched him grow. He was a quiet, sensitive boy, easily managed. It wasn't long until she found him out in the byre following George and Johnny, stroking the young calves, gathering eggs, and pulling the cat's tail. She began to rely on him for some simple chores and George had to do less walking.

Like all the others, her eighth child was no mistake.

Chapter 2

The morning was a busy one in Anne's kitchen. Children and babies were in and out along with an occasional hapless chicken promptly chased by the boys.

Earlier it had misted, then cleared with a rainbow dancing over the lough. Now the sun poured in the east window like warm gold. Outside the window a pink rosebush bloomed and over by the chicken house was an overgrown fuchsia bobbing in the wind.

Maggie Moore had just stopped by on her way to Creeslough. She found Anne surrounded by a mountain of laundry and a big pot full of white shirts boiling over the fire to whiten them.

"Aye, surely I'm glad to be seeing ye, Maggie," said Anne as she scrubbed the clothes on her washboard. Anne liked the feel of warm water and soap, the odor of wet clothes, the pure whiteness of the boiled linens. And she always liked to have a neighbor drop in.

"How's this wee boy doing since I was last here?" asked Maggie, knowing that Sandy had never been all that well since she helped deliver him months before. She lifted him out of the cradle and sat with him on her lap.

"He seems rightly the day, but there's no telling, Maggie. Of them all, he seems the frailest," and Anne scrubbed the clothes a little harder. She loved her children, all eleven of them, and not one could she spare. In her heart was always a nagging

11

fear about this little boy, the smallest and most delicate. Her milk had always agreed with her babies and they had grown like young potato plants in June, but Sandy had trouble digesting it and complained so much.

"Maggie, will ye have a cup o' tae? James, go and get some water from the well. I have none left."

James, feeling mature and experienced from his year in school, picked up a small bucket and swinging it easily, ran down the lane, scattering chickens as he ran, shouting at George who was helping Robert clean the byre this morning.

The lane went down around a bend, rutted and muddy from all the rain this wet summer. James skipped, awkwardly and merrily. He avoided the deeper holes, listened to a thrush sing, and reached the well in moments.

It was not more than three feet deep, actually a spring caught in a hole that had been enlarged by digging and the sides supported by stone work. Above was a flag stone across it to keep out leaves, cow manure, and careless animals who might fall in. There was just enough room to reach in with a bucket and pull it out. Always it was a soggy low place.

James reached in at the side holding on to the flag with one hand and leaning down with his small bucket to fill it. Suddenly the flag slipped and he fell in head first. The water was shockingly cold. He gasped in surprise, drawing the water into his nose. In terror he flailed with his arms, his legs, but there wasn't room to turn. The water burned his nose, his lungs exploded, he kicked wildly, his bare knees hit a stone, and suddenly his head was out of the water, how he never knew.

For a moment he was still, gasping, breathing heavily, too surprised to move, knowing he was alive at least. Then he realized he was cold. He had to get out. By sheer will power he pulled himself up the slippery side and out into the slimy mud at the opening. Later he was to wonder how he had done it.

He ran heavily back up the lane. The air blew keenly against him and he shook with fear and cold.

Anne, who had begun to wonder why he was so long, stood at the door and saw him coming around the corner past the fuchsia bush. Johnny saw him too. "Look at him, Mammy," he chuckled.

"Quate, the weane could have drowned," said Anne sharply. She gathered him into her arms, mud and all, and took him to the fire.

"Ah, wee man, what happened, did ye fall in, my wee boy," she crooned, as she took off his soaking clothes. James shook with sobs now, the warmth and his mother's words melting the barricade of courage and will that had sustained him.

The family, curious, had gathered around. Mary came with dry pants and a warm jersey. His mother wrapped him in a blanket and held him on her lap by the fire. Annie Jane was sent to get more water for the tea with strict instructions to be careful.

Maggie, the visitor, had sat patiently throughout. She was holding Sandy and taking in the whole episode to tell it later at the co-op when she would finally get to Creeslough.

The tea was soon made and James received the first cup with an extra big slice of scone and fresh-made butter that Anne had churned that morning. He had never had so much attention and he sat smiling, cozily comforted by the tea and his mother's lap, half listening to the grown up talk and feeling sleepy.

He remembered the prayer, "If I should die before I wake, I pray thee, Lord, my soul to take." He had nearly died. Even at age six he knew how close he had come. The paralyzing fear swept over him again and he shivered.

"Still cold?" asked Mary. He shook his head.

He privately resolved to say his prayers that night more fervently than ever before, "Now I lay me" and "Our Father." These were the two which his mother had instructed him to pray every night by his bed. And with a strange longing inside, James always did, kneeling in the chilly attic room beside the bed he shared with George and young Thomas. The others didn't always remember, but James knew he would never forget again.

Anne pondered that day often in the next months. She told John about it when he came home from Derry on Saturday where he had been working that week.

John was not unduly perturbed. This multitude of squirming youngsters he had sired confused him when he thought about them too much. The older ones he knew fairly well, the younger ones scarcely at all. He was seldom with them, never without several at once, always with noise and perpetual motion.

Yet that same evening he went to the back potato field to watch the boys work. Robert on a cart was dumping manure here and there while James and George with dung forks spread it evenly over the field. He considered James more closely. He was long and thin for his age with a thicket of wavy hair the color of ripe wheat and with a natural bent for farm work. John Hay prided himself on his ability to work hard and fast. He wanted his sons to do the same. It was the best he could give them.

Back at the house, he said to Anne, "He's a good worker, James is."

"Aye, he is," said Anne, as she busily mixed a scone. "And he's good to the younger ones too."

But John wasn't listening. He picked up a Dublin paper and settled himself in the corner by the fire.

"The house could burn down and ye'd burn with it," said Anne as she put the scone in a large black pan. She was tired this long summer evening. Yet she knew that John had come home again with his thirty shillings and given a good portion of it to her for the needs at home. John was reliable and steady, a good provider, honest and respected.

So Anne thought as she built up the fire and hung the pan of scone on the crane over the coals, put the lid on, and laid live coals of turf on top of the lid to bake the bread through.

She sat to mend half a dozen pair of pants, sorting through to see how and where to begin. One, a pair of George's, had been worn probably by four boys, and even the patches were torn. A proverb of her mother's came to mind and she smiled

14

saying it half aloud, "Patches beside patches is neighborly, but patches upon patches is beggarly." This pair was good only for washing the floor.

Later when the children gathered around for their supper of broughen, Anne saw a tired, drawn look on the face of Madge who was quieter than usual. Anne's heart softened. Her eldest daughter must be growing into womanhood. She would speak to her when there was a moment of solitude, a rare thing but she must arrange it.

That evening when the family was in bed, Anne crept into the tiny bedroom shared by Madge and Annie Jane.

"Mammy, I can't sleep," said Madge.

"What's wrong, wee dear?"

"There's a sore place on me back," said Madge. "I can't lie that way, only on me side."

"Let me see," said Anne. She set the candle on the chair and looked at the soft white skin in the exquisite hollow of her back. There was a slightly raised spot on Madge's spine and when she pressed it, Madge gasped.

"Oh, Mammy, that hurts. Don't touch it," she said. Her eyes in the dim light were big and dark with pain and fear.

"How long has it been there?" asked Anne.

"I don't know. A good wee while, but it didn't hurt much at first. It's bigger now."

"Does it hurt all the time or only when I touch it?"

"I'm not sure. I—I think it hurts all the time. It seems to be getting worse."

"Try to sleep on your side. I'll put a poultice on it tomorrow and that should help it come to a head," said Anne. She patted Madge's face, covered her, and crept into her own bed. There wasn't time for more than a brief prayer before she was asleep.

But the poultice didn't help and Madge looked more ashen. Anne knew the pain was worse though the girl seldom complained. She went to school as usual and helped with the little ones, especially small Sandy. The two of them would sit together,

15

Madge rocking the little boy and singing a song before the fire.

Anne knew she was always tired. The child would have to stay home from school and try to get her strength, she decided. John agreed with her.

"I don't know how else to help her," said Anne in a discouraged tone.

"We'll take her to the doctor," said John.

Anne looked at him swiftly. To the doctor? She had nursed children through all kinds of fever and flu, even wee Thomas through the diphtheria. He had made it even when several neighbor children had died. John must think Madge very ill indeed to take her to the doctor. Could it be he feared the same thing she did?

When they went, the doctor's breath smelled like whiskey. He told Anne to keep using the poultices except to add a salve that he gave her. And keep her warm, he said.

Anne borrowed a hot-water bottle to put in Madge's bed at night. That lower bedroom was chilly and the bed damp. It gave Madge some comfort but brought no change to her back.

As the dark winter with cold, short days reluctantly turned into spring, Anne breathed in relief. Surely with the weather changing, Madge would improve. The sun would drive away this illness, as it did the coughs and chest colds of all the others. Winter was always a risky time with weanes. Thank God, they had all survived the bleak months again.

Outside snowdrops bloomed in small cracks along the wall away from the wind where the sun warmed the earth. Next came primroses in May and suddenly the park was filled with the glory of golden whins. The bushes, prickly and useless except for draping wet clothes there to dry, were covered with a multitude of brilliant yellow blooms lighting up even the cloudy days. The pink rosebush was in bud and the boys were planting the fields.

One fair morning Anne had come in from an inspection of the farm with Robert and Johnny. They were finished planting the potatoes and Anne told them where to put some cabbage. As she came into the kitchen, she heard sobbing.

There was Madge crying with Sandy beside her, a small frown on his face as he leaned against his sister's leg and peered earnestly at her face.

"What is it, Cutye?" asked Anne with a tight feeling around her heart.

"Oh, Mammy, me legs hurt so bad I can't stand it."

"When did this start?" asked Anne.

"A—a few days ago. I didn't want to be telling ye, but it's getting worse."

Anne stopped beside Madge and rubbed her legs. She knew there was nothing, nothing she could do. The illness was getting worse. Sunshine would not cure this inward lump. It would grow and twist and finally squeeze the life from this girl, this first-born daughter.

"Do something, Mammy," pleaded Madge.

"I will surely," said Anne.

But what? What was she to do? The doctor couldn't help. When John came home that next evening, he looked sober as he saw Madge huddled by the fire, a blanket around her legs, rocking in misery.

"We better try the hospital, Anne," he said.

There was no hope then, Anne knew. Hospitals were for the dying. Numbly she gathered up a few clothes, and she and John took Madge to the train station. She kissed her daughter and said cheerily, "You'll soon be better at the hospital, Tutsie. There must be doctors there that can help ye."

John went with her to the hospital and Anne went slowly back up the road to Rooskey in the long twilight, her heart as heavy as the cows' udders waiting to be milked.

She must hurry. Robert had been working in the turf all day and needed his supper. When she reached the house, she found Maggie Moore there giving the boys tea and smiling them into some kind of cheerfulness.

17

Anne sat down gratefully with a cup of tea and a piece of scone that Maggie had brought. Annie Jane sat beside her and little Sandy crawled up on her lap. Thank God, he was a bit better now. Her thoughts encircled the hospital at Lifford. Was Madge afraid? Did she know she was probably dying? Would John remember to linger with her awhile before he came home? When did the last train come? Probably he would stay all night and come on Sunday.

John came, late at night, walking home from the station. Anne, in the darkness of their room, said, "Is that you, John?"

"Aye."

"How is she?"

"She's a sick wee girl, Anne. Only God knows how sick."

He crawled in beside her and put his arms around her and held her tightly. For Anne was sobbing and she discovered that John's tears were mixed with hers. They wept together and fell asleep in a tenderness they had nearly forgotten.

Chapter 3

It was three weeks later that James and George, coming back with the cows over baighy, saw the cart coming up the Rooskey Road.

"There they are," said George.

"Aye, let's run," said James giving the cows a whack with the stick which sent them lumbering down the hill, across the road, and into the street to the byre. The milking would have to be done, but it could wait. John and Anne with Madge drove the cart in beside the door and helped Madge get out. She could not stand alone, so Robert and Johnny each took an arm and supported her into bed.

James watched, round-eyed. He saw his mother's grim face. "Did the hospital help Madge, Mammy?" asked George.

"No, they didn't. But we'll take care of her here," she said. "Make some tea for the weane, Johnny."

George and Robert unhitched the horse, then did the milking. James watched them, running occasionally into the kitchen to see what was happening there and reporting back to his brothers.

"Madge looks white, whiter than anyone I ever saw," he said.

"Will she get well?" asked George.

"I don't know," said Robert. He had his own thoughts, but he wouldn't tell these two. He had seen the sorrow in Anne's eyes.

Fair Day in Creeslough.

The summer went by with more sunshine than usual. The children played and worked with their usual high spirits. By now Willie was working in Derry at the Port, educating himself at night classes. Robert and Johnny cut and dried the turf, thinned turnips, cut hay. The high point of the season was the Lamas Fair in Creeslough, the biggest fair of the year, held in August. Anne had two calves to sell, but this year she couldn't go. Robert would have to manage the sale alone.

Madge was weaker each day and Anne wouldn't leave her very long at a time. When the Fair Day came, the family went merrily down the road while silence fell upon the house like a soft blanket. Outside a blackbird warbled its sweet song on the fuchsia bush heavy with royal purple blossoms.

Anne was baking, knowing that a hungry family would return that evening. She moved heavily. Lamas Fair was one of her favorite days, the time of harvest and rejoicing. She always loved seeing friends, haggling over the price of calves or pigs, having tea with the Gallaghers, watching her children run happily about, each with a penny to buy gooseberries.

But this year she worked quietly in the kitchen, knowing that

20

the death-angel waited outside the door. Always there just out of sight and reach, but his shadow in plain view, waiting to come and take this thin, helpless, pain-racked daughter.

"Mammy, give me some tea," said Madge.

"Aye, Tutsie."

Madge seldom asked for anything and ate next to nothing. Anne put a bit of bread on the plate hoping the girl would eat it, watching her from the corner of her eye while she patted the scone into the kettle to bake over the fire.

"Mammy, will I die?" she asked later.

Anne stopped and looked at her. She couldn't lie. "Madge, me cutye, I don't know. You're wild sick."

"Aye. I won't be well ever again. I don't think I want to be. I'm too tired."

"Are ye afraid?" asked Anne.

"No, Mammy, I say me prayers often and I'm not afraid." Her eyes looked steadily at Anne who sighed in relief. So often she had wondered and worried about that. It was a small comfort on this dark day to know that Margery was not afraid.

It was the only time they ever spoke together of the inexorable event that couldn't be far away now. Madge got slowly weaker and couldn't sit up at all, and the vicious pain declined. Anne thanked God for that.

In September the children started school again. There was great confusion and commotion as everyone gathered copybooks and packed a dry piece of scone in their bags for lunch. Rebecca began the infants' class, tagging along with James, who felt competent and responsible. A few days into the term, Anne knew that Madge's time was near.

She watched her that day with Sandy and Thomas close at her heels, in and out of Madge's room. Should she send for John? He wouldn't be home til Saturday.

As the day wore on, Madge went to sleep, but she lay so still that Anne at first thought she was gone. Maggie Moore stopped by.

"There's na' much time left, Anne," she said. "Do ye want my Willie to go for John?"

Anne nodded. Waves of sorrow rolled over her. She wanted to grip Margery and hold her tight against this thing that waited to snatch her daughter, this gentle lass who had loved Sandy and helped Anne countless times.

That evening, late, John came. Neighbors dropped in and sat hushed around the fire. Maggie helped with the children and the boys did the chores without being reminded.

Anne sat by Madge's bed, holding her hand, watching the rise and fall of her breast. Sometimes it seemed to be stopped and then it would start again.

All these years she had known she would lose one. When Sandy was born, weak and small, she was sure it would be he. Hardly any woman she knew had got eleven children through infancy, that treacherous first year when a baby could be gone over the sake of a fever or the wrong food or even a malignant fairy. Hers had survived, all of them, only to come to this.

Madge—her oldest daughter, with her sweet maturity, the thick wavy hair, her body filling out into womanhood, oh, God, not this one. But which one then could she spare? How absurd, how dreadful to consider one she could give up. No matter what the pain of child-bearing, no matter the poverty or hardship, Anne could not spare one.

Madge stirred ever so slightly, gasping, then relaxing the hold on Anne's hand. She was leaving, Anne knew. The breathing was faint, fluttering.

There was nothing now but submission. No good railing against the Creator, God the Lord.

And by an act of her will, Anne let Madge go. She couldn't hold the girl in the pain and frailty of this life. Better to yield to the merciful hands of God. And with that, the child was gone.

John, beside her, leaned his head on his hands. Anne put her arm around him. John, her strong husband, shook with the silent sobs that rack men in the grip of a terrible grief, and she knew he had loved this girl perhaps more than any of the others. A man wants a son, but adores his daughters. This, the first one, had a singular place in his heart.

"We must go, John, and tell the others," she said.

They walked through the sitting room and into the kitchen where neighbors had lingered though it was late. They would stay all night and for the next three days, coming and going, drinking and eating with the family, never leaving them completely alone. The Irish wake was a time of support, a sharing of grief, without hurry. The dead were respected, the living comforted.

James, small and unsure of the implications of all that happened, enjoyed all the company, the excitement, the food. For once, he ate whenever he felt like it. He and George had raisin scone until they were sated, two little boys cheerfully making the most of all they could lay hands on. When evening came, he sat on his stool, thoroughly satisfied, leaning his head against the wall where he would fall fast asleep. Johnny or Robert carried him off to bed.

But it came to an end with the funeral, and then a dreadful awareness of death came to him. This was the end of Madge, his sister. Where had she gone? To Heaven, they said. Where was that? He had seen her lying in her coffin in the sitting room, but now she was in the ground. How ever did she get to Heaven? He remembered the time he had nearly drowned. Would he have gone to Heaven, to God? He had a strange yearning in his heart, to know the way, to be sure of he knew not what. Would he ever see Madge again?

He thought of all his small sins, the unkind words, the bad thoughts, the times he hit Thomas or Rebecca. Would these keep him from Heaven? He felt soiled, unclean, unfit.

That night at bedtime as he knelt to pray the "Our Father" and "Now I lay me," he felt as though he should do more. He waited a moment, then remembered the verse from a hymn that he liked.

Jesus, my Lord, I thee adore,
Help me to love thee more and more.

He would pray that every night. He liked the sound of it, the flow of the words. That would help. Praying would surely help him get to Heaven.

He fell asleep beside George in the loft bed, a single star showing through the one tiny window on his face.

Chapter 4

The school years stretched interminably before James as he reached the fourth class. He was quick enough at learning and even enjoyed it on occasion, especially the lessons from history, the Bible stories, the legends and literature of Ireland and Britain, even math. But there were such long waits, hours of sitting with his pencil practicing penmanship, up, down, up, down, meeting the red lines for the large letters, the blue lines for the small ones, hours of listening to recitations of other classes, studying his spelling words and math facts, and hours of just sitting and wishing he could run and dig potatoes and chase cows. School was so comfortless and dreary, and home was warm, bright, and free.

One cheerless, midwinter day the crowd of little Hays and Moores arrived scrappily at the schoolyard, each carrying a piece of turf to burn in the fire that day. All along the way to school they had bickered about marbles and who was the best player. At lunch time they would play again and decide on the champion.

James sat at his desk with Tommy Moore. His feet were cold and he was too far from the fire to hope for any warmth this morning. After the religious instruction with a story about Jacob and Esau, Tommy nudged James.

"James, let me have your copybook."

James looked carefully from the corner of his eye at Miss

Wilkinson, busy with the fifth class. Tommy's page was empty. He had trouble with long division. It was difficult enough for James too, but George, who was good at mathematics, had helped him sometimes.

"Here ye be, Tommy," he said.

"James," said Miss Wilkinson.

James jumped. He'd get it now, surely to goodness, the stick that she kept in the corner.

"Aye," he said timidly, his soft hazel eyes suddenly intense.

But she only said, "Would you and Tommy get the water please?"

Would they! That was always a sought-after diversion, and Tommy was just the one to do it with. He was naturally slow, and a boy could spend a good half-hour or more getting the water with him.

Trying to keep the smug smiles off their faces and failing utterly, they grabbed their caps and hurried out the door with the bucket. Finley hissed something at James as he went by, but he didn't stop to listen. He guessed Finley, who liked to pick fights, was angry because he hadn't been chosen this time.

The penetrating chill of midwinter, the lightly falling rain, the bare legs and short pants, none of this could quench the warmth these two felt as they gleefully walked along the road into Creeslough to the well. On the way they fondled their marbles, counting and comparing them. James had a goodly number, considering it was war days when everything was as scarce as a hen's tooth. Tommy eyed them wistfully.

"I loss mine when I play," he said.

"I'll help ye," said James. "My brothers showed me how to play. I've won most of mine."

"Aye, thon blue one is mine and that nice yellow one." Tommy knew James was a good player and often came away with extra ones.

They reached the well and filled the bucket. Coming back up the slippery, wet steps, James, still as awkward as a young giraffe, tripped over his long feet and spilled half of it.

He looked at Tommy and grinned. "We'll have to get some more, Tommy."

"Aye, we will surely," agreed Tommy.

So even more slowly they walked down the steps, filled the bucket again, pulled it up, and set off with no more than a few minor splashes along the way. Their feet were damp, but then it was rare to have feet completely dry.

At the school they crept in quietly, hoping Miss Wilkinson wouldn't recollect how long they'd been. She was fortunately distracted by Finley just at that moment, Finley who was born to trouble as the sparks fly upward.

James slid into his seat after slinging his cap neatly onto the ledge along with the others. He remembered his promise to Tommy to help him with marbles. Reaching into his pocket, he held his and caressed them slowly, listening to them squeak against each other. They were beauties, he thought, and he had more than nearly any other boy. He and George spent hours playing on rainy days, and he had learned all the tricks of the game.

Tommy whispered, "Let me see them again, James."

James held them out in his none-too-clean hand. Tommy touched them gently, lovingly.

"Will ye really help me, James?" he asked.

James nodded reassuringly. At that moment a quick hand swooped down from behind and snatched his marbles like a magpie stealing a young chick. Miss Wilkinson had walked up the aisle with a gleam in her eye and seen the sparkling marbles in that outstretched hand. James clutched at her arm, but she shook him off. George, sitting across the aisle, sucked in his breath involuntarily and wondered what James would do. He **loved** marbles.

"I'll keep them for you, James, til the end of the term," said Miss Wilkinson crisply. "Then you won't be using them in school."

27

Til the end of the term—why, that was months away. James felt his face go hot and his hand, still outstretched, trembled. He sat back and put his hand in his empty pocket. It couldn't be. Just seconds ago it had been full, bulging with smooth, shiny marbles.

Tommy looked at him guiltily. "I'm sorry, James," he said.

James nodded dumbly. His eyes were filling with tears but he was too big to cry. His little brother Thomas could cry, but not him. He shook the tears away, looked wrathfully at Miss Wilkinson's straight, determined back, and then down at his copybook of long division.

Tommy needed it to copy. He hadn't got his work done yet. James handed it over with his face averted and opened his spelling lesson blindly. It would be a long, long time til he had marbles again.

At lunch he stood in a corner of the schoolyard and pretended to watch something down the road, a cartload of squealing pigs. George came to him and said he could use his marbles for a game but not for keeps, but James shook his head.

When school was over at last, he rushed home ahead of the others. It was no fun to loiter along the way with the Moores when his heart hurt and his pockets were empty. In the kitchen his mother sat with three-year-old Sandy on her lap by the fire.

"How's my wee man?" she said.

"Oh, Mammy," he began, then burst into sobs. Anne held him against her.

"There now, wee man, there now," she murmured to him rubbing his springy fair hair.

He cried himself out and was only sniffling as the others came and told the story. Anne did not believe in giving sympathy to naughty children, but neither did she think a teacher should be cruel. James could have borne a beating easier than the loss of his treasures.

But Anne held her peace. She set the potatoes on the table and watched her hungry children eat like young wolves, noisily, quickly. Then she made a pot of hot, strong tea for them. On this mist-penetrating day they needed the warmth. The kitchen smelled of damp woolen clothes and the fire sizzled and popped as tea boiled over on the hob. The group at the table was noisier than ever as their stomachs filled and they relaxed in the warmth. James was eating in a half-hearted way. Anne knew how he hurt, and her heart ached too. A small thing perhaps in a lifetime of aches, but to one little boy it was a calamity.

She sat beside him on the bench and whispered in his ear. "Tomorrow I need a boy to help me get ready for the Fair Day."

His mouth full of scone and tea, James nodded happily. His eyes shone and the worried look left his brow.

That meant two whole days off school, for the day after tomorrow was the Fair Day in Creeslough, and no one went to school then. Anne squeezed his hand. James smiled and followed George outside, down the street, and through the lane to the meadow to get the cows.

A typical Irish farmhouse kitchen.

Chapter 5

Spring comes subtly in a land that is green all the year. Yet the air lightens and warms gradually and wildflowers spring up. At Rooskey as the days lengthened, the young Hays fairly bounced with energy and enthusiasm.

It was May, one of the loveliest of months. Though George had stayed the day before, James, on this day, was allowed to remain home from school and keep the cows out of the crops. With his bad foot, his brother had to go to school more regularly. For this James could only be thankful.

The morning was brilliant, with a false brilliance, the kind of day that Anne said ended up in rain.

James happily herded the two cows and one heifer down to the lough field. The top half of the field had potatoes peeping through the ground, young tender plants in neat rows of green. His job was to keep the cows from trampling these plants into oblivion. He and the animals had to stay in the grassy lower part of the field. No one knew about putting a barbed wire around a field for a few weeks, and there was no money to buy it had they known. Boys were plentiful and cost very little. They could keep the cows where they belonged.

James sat still for awhile beside the lough, skipping pebbles across the smooth, gleaming water with an alert eye on the cows behind him. As soon as they ventured toward the potatoes, he ran with his stick, laughing to see them clumsily run down the hill again nearer to the lough.

It was peaceful here by the water, too peaceful, and James soon grew lonely. He listened to several birds sing and found two nests. By the lough he tried to hit a fish with a stone, then lost his balance and fell against a nettle. His leg tingled for the next hour. After two hours he was ravenously hungry and tired of his own company.

His mother with little Sandy appeared. "James," she called, "bring the cows up the street and I'll give ye a bit of bread and tea. Then take them to the hill pasture."

He obeyed with alacrity, walking with Anne, holding Sandy's hand, back up the lane rutted with hoofs, past the well into which he had fallen, past the small garden and the byre where he left the cows, then into the kitchen. It was a sunny day but still cool, and the warm fire felt good though his hands with the chilblains itched uncomfortably. Sandy climbed up on the bench beside him and James smiled at him companionably.

"Take the cows to the hill, James," said Anne. "Leave them and come help me churn til milking time."

After his tea, he gathered the cows and went about a mile away to the foothills of Muckish, the mountain that dominated the countryside. James looked at the mountain looming ahead of him, stolid, immovable, and he saw a cloud forming over it. That meant rain.

"James."

It was Mickey, sitting on a wall watching his cattle in his own father's hill field. "James, stay with me a wee while."

James understood. It was a desperately lonesome spot, no houses nearby, ony a few sheep and cattle on this wind-swept high pasture. And who knew how many wee folk lived in these heather-thick hills, in the rocks, through the deep grass?

"I'd better be going home, Mickey," he said doubtfully. "Mammy wants me to help churn."

"Ach, James, stay with me. I'll give ye a penny," he said hopefully.

A penny. What he couldn't do with a penny. Where did Mickey get an extra penny? He guessed that he, being older, had earned it somehow. He must be rich indeed if he could give a penny away.

"Let me see it," demanded James.

Mickey got the penny, polished it against his pants, then held it high for James to see. It was a real penny all right. The only time James ever got one was for the Lamas Fair in August, or sometimes Willie gave him one when he came home from his job in Derry.

He reached for it. "I'll stay," he said briefly.

They sat amicably, watching the cows before them, talking occasionally, but mostly just sitting, enjoying the company all the better for being so uncommon on these barren hills. In the distance James could see the sea with the steel gray sky reflecting heavily on it. The brilliant morning had long since gone, and a heaviness was in the air.

Several hours went by. Suddenly James heard thunder. Storms were uncommon and he feared them. He must go. What would his mother say that he had stayed so long?

"I have to go, Mickey," he said. "Mammy will be cross."

He began to herd his cows together. The sky was blacker now and Muckish was completely covered by a cloud. Beyond Downings he could see lightning flash in the sky and he heard the low growl of offended deities that lived beyond the clouds. The fairies hissed in the wildly blowing grass as the wind careened in from the west.

James was on the hillside alone with a storm and all the elements around him growing wilder by the moment. Mickey had already fled.

He yelled at the cows, using his stick to prod them back to the path. His only thought was to get home as quickly as possible to his mother sitting behind the door praying.

With a roar he chased the cows down the hillside. The rain came on hard, blowing straight into his face, drenching him in seconds, but he rushed on, hitting at the cow before him. The cows, terrified from the weather and the wild banshee shouting at their heels, lumbered along, their full udders swaying heavily, one of them large with an unborn calf, past the tiny hillside farms, on to the rutted road. The merciless boy pursued them, chasing, hitting, running faster and faster.

James never stopped until he reached the lane into his home. There he let the cows make their own way to the byre while he rushed to the door. It was closed, the only time he could remember being outside that closed door, for it always stood open summer and winter.

"Mammy, Mammy, let me in," he called, banging on the door. "There's a wild big plump."

Anne opened it a crack and pulled him in, putting her arm around him though he was dripping.

Then she sat again, behind the door with Sandy on her lap, a good grip on James, and the others crowded around as close as possible til the storm passed by. Only then did they move and speak again.

Later when his mother asked, he told her the cows were running with the heat and he had to stay in the hill with them. But George, listening, knew he lied.

That evening by the fire, James sat and pondered. He hadn't listened to his mother that day. Then to compound the disobedience, he had told her a lie. It lay heavy on his conscience. He thought of his sister Mary who had been attending some meetings at Brocas recently. James had been curious about the meetings especially since he had seen a difference in Mary. She was gentler with him, for one thing, and she seemed to be always singing. Of all the happy Hays, she was the most joyful, the one who sang while she worked. It made James wonder, and the old familiar yearning came back. There was something he didn't know, something he longed to know with all his heart, but he couldn't have expressed it to save his life.

And so, two nights before the storm when Finley Kearney

34

came by the house and whispered that he was going to George the preacher's house that evening and would James like to go along, James said yes without hesitation. He did not tell his mother his plans (she looked askance at the strange group meeting at Brocas since the Hays were members in good standing at the Church of Ireland), merely saying that he and Finley would walk to Magheroarty that evening and maybe stop at the preacher's house on the way. His mother made no queries. He was old enough to walk about on a long light spring evening, and with the house full of people all the time, he was hardly missed.

At the meeting he spied Mary waiting for the service to begin. He and Finley slipped in quietly, giggling self-consciously at first, then settling to listen. They sang hymns, easy, lively tunes that he could learn after hearing them once. He joined in with a half-shy glance at Finley who still felt silly. It moved along cheerfully, and there was a warmth that James had never felt at a church service. They read no collects, recited no prayers, did nothing to which he was accustomed, yet there was spontaneity and joy. Mary smiled at him and he knew she was glad to see him there. He also knew she would not tell on him.

When the speaker stood to preach, Finley was squirming from sitting too long, but James resisted his pressure to leave just then. He wanted to stay and listen. Maybe he would find out why Mary smiled so much.

Now, two nights later, James remembered little of the message except the text. He had a penchant for memorizing anything rhythmical or poetic. "Many lepers were in Israel but only Naaman was healed by Elias." It was a strange verse. Why would God heal one leper and not another, he wondered. Did God love one person more than another? Was that fair? But then, God was—well, God. He didn't know if he, James Hay of Rooskey, could query God.

Did God know he'd lied that day? It weighed on him. And there were many other times when he had sinned. What could

35

he do about it? He must try harder not to sin, yet that which he'd done already was still there.

He was tired. It was too much to think about, and he trudged off to say his prayers and go to bed.

Chapter 6

One of the biggest projects of each summer in Donegal was cutting the turf and bringing it home for the year's supply of fuel. Neighbors worked together and all the family joined in to help.

Thus the Hays were up early one gray June morning with a damp wind blowing in from the east. Hugh Whorskey and John William Mickey were to come for breakfast to eat with Robert, as the custom was, before the three of them set out for the bog to cut the Hays' turf.

James watched his mother prepare the food. She had saved duck eggs for a couple weeks for this occasion. Only duck eggs could be served to bog men.

"Mammy, could I have one?"

"Haul' your tongue, these are for the men," she said. "Get the plain and raisin scones from the pantry."

James went into one of the two tiny rooms behind the kitchen, the one from which he climbed the stairs each night to his bed. He found the scones covered with a cloth on the bread board, baked just yesterday. Raisin scone on a **Tuesday.** He picked a couple raisins off the top and munched them appreciatively.

"James, be leaving that scone alone," called Anne.

"Don't you want me to bring it?" he asked innocently.

"Quiet, weane, do what ye're told," Anne said distractedly. Thomas and Sandy were bickering over some marbles, the girls weren't helping like they should, and Hugh and Johnnie were already arriving at the door for their breakfast.

She gave the boys a swat across their ears, told Annie Jane to get some more water, then cut up the scones.

"Sit down, Hugh and Johnnie. Here's your tea. Robert, set ye here."

The family stood back, watching hungrily til the men were done. Eating never took long in Ireland. Plain food with no adornment, it was meant for nourishment, not for lingering over. The men pushed back their chairs, thanked Anne, and went outside where their shovels and spades leaned by the house.

They began the two-mile walk along the winding, rocky road to the Hay bog in the shadow of Muckish. Robert enjoyed working there as long as it didn't rain. A steady drizzle could make a man cold to his bones. He didn't especially like the feel of the wind today. It was raw and could bring on the rain, he knew.

At the bog, marking off the area, the three men set to digging. First they took off the layer of thick grass and heather growth, then using sharp L-shaped spades, began to cut vertically into the bog. Digging, cutting, lifting the water-logged turf, and finally spreading it out to dry. It was back-breaking work hour after damp hour.

For Robert's intuition had been right and a mist swept down off Muckish, steeping them in chilly misery. Their feet were damp from the water in the bog.

There was no break all morning while they worked steadily. Then a cheery call came and looking up, they saw James and Mary leading the donkey loaded with food. There were hot, boiled potatoes wrapped in a newspaper and a woolen blanket, three more duck eggs for each man, scones and butter.

The mist had stopped now and a lemon-colored sun was shining. Sitting by the small fire, the men devoured the warm food, watched anxiously by James. Robert gave him a boiled potato but no egg. He ate it and wished for more. Mary made tea on the fire.

Warmed and sustained by food, the three men relaxed a few minutes after they finished eating. Robert smoked his pipe.

Their shoes steamed a little by the fire.

Then Robert got up slowly and the other two followed. James and Mary put the girth and creels back on the donkey, who had been contentedly grazing along the road, and walked back home.

Through the afternoon the men kept on digging, cutting, lifting, spreading out the soft mushy turf to dry. The square trenches where they had dug were already half full of water. It had been a wet spring.

They had stopped for tea around 4 p.m. Heating water on the small fire, they made a pot of strong tea and drank it along with the scone left over from dinner.

It was late in the long evening when they slowly walked back to the Hays' house. The kitchen was warm and the lamp burning. Anne had made a big pot of porridge and gave each man a bowl before they separated for the night.

Robert sat back and sighed. His feet, still encased in the damp shoes, felt warm by the fire.

"Nearly too wet to cut," he said to his mother. "Should be getting better though as we go on. Hugh's bog is higher than ours and won't be so bad."

"Aye, I hope so," said Anne. It had been a long hard day, she knew.

Robert fell into bed that night, bathless, without clean clothes, for one changed only once a week. The next morning the ritual was repeated—duck eggs, raisin scone, and tea, then off to work. This would go on for nine days, the men working three days for each of their families, cutting thousands of pieces of turf to warm them and to cook their food for another year.

Ten days later in early July, Anne said, "It's time you weanes were off and turned the turf."

The next morning George, James, and Mary set off along the road with a lunch of dry scone and some tea to make at the bog. No duck eggs for children.

It was hard, boring work, stooping low all day and turning

39

each piece of turf, hundreds of them, so it could dry on the other side. This day was bright with wonderful cloud shadows moving across the bog like dark ships. The sky, like a blue cup inverted above them, poured warm sunshine on their backs all day. The work went quickly, at least through the morning, but by noon every muscle ached though they knew they couldn't go home. Their movements slowed and became automatic.

At the end of the day there was still some work to be finished. They would have to come back in the morning again, notwithstanding sore muscles.

And yet the work in the bog was only half completed. A week later the children returned again, more of them this time, small Rebecca learning to work with her brothers, and Mary along to keep them all in order. This time they stood each turf on end, five pieces leaning against each other in tent-like shapes called rickles, the last stage of drying. It didn't seem quite so tiring, but it took longer.

James helped Rebecca. He was fond of this little sister of his. She looked mighty small to be here working all day.

"Did you know, Tutsie, that there be fairies here?" he asked.

Her gray eyes got big. "Where?" she whispered.

"I'll show ye," he said drawing her away from the others. "You see yon rock over there? Well, behind it Andy says they live."

"Did ye see them, James?" she asked.

"No, but I've heard them. On windy days ye can hear them sing. And evenings, ye can see them, but I never did. I make sure I leave early enough, so's I don't."

Rebecca nodded solemnly. She would make sure she left when James did so she wouldn't see them either. A fairy was, well, a fairy, unpredictable, sometimes kind, but more often malicious. You could never trust a fairy.

James chuckled to himself. He remembered a story his usually serious father told with relish, how coming home years earlier as a young man from a dance, he had climbed late at night to a rock in Barnesmore Gap, a forsaken place even in daylight. There he had sat in the darkness and played an accordian, terrifying those who passed by from the same dance.

By now James was outgrowing his fear of fairies, yet it was true that at twilight people did seem to see strange things. In the mist and fog of a long summer evening or early in the morning there was no accounting for the strange visions and sounds neighbors reported. His mother, he knew, firmly believed in the wee folk though he doubted if his down-to-earth father did.

The day passed and two more before the turf was all rickled. The children were relieved to be finished with the work. But two weeks later Anne told them to get the donkey and creels and go again to the bog. There Johnnie, George, and James hauled the turf all day from the bog to the edge of the road where they stacked it. It made an enormous pile and Robert had to go the second day to help them get it high enough. Then he and Johnnie came with the horse and cart and began to haul it slowly to the house. There they stacked it against the north wall of the house which had no windows.

From the time of the first cutting til they brought it all home, the turf took the most of two months, allowing time for all the vagaries of the weather. As the cart came creaking in through the gate with the last load, Anne was there to meet them. She smiled at Robert as he led the weary horse while the boys walked beside the cart, balancing it as it made the precarious turn into the lane.

"Thank God, we'll be warm again the winter," she said. "Ye've been a good help, weanes. Come in for your tea."

And that was the end of the turf harvest for another year.

The Hay Family, left to right, back row: Rebecca, George, James, Thomas, and Mary; front row: John (father), Sandy, and Anne (mother).

Chapter 7

As the years went by, life got easier for the Hays with several members away from home earning money. But there were crises, too, heartaches which inevitably accompany such a large family. Willie, the oldest went off to war. He fought in the trenches of France, and then was heard from no more. Anne was sure he was dead, but he finally returned after many long months as a gaunt prisoner of war. Never would he speak of his experiences even to her. (Years later when World War II began, he sat and wept to hear the news.)

Willie began to work again in Derry, Johnnie had a job in Belfast, and Robert helped at the Baxter's place, relatives of the Hays.

Thus it fell on James to stay home from school more and more, plowing, planting, taking more responsibility from his mother. He liked farming. Watching young James plow one day, a neighbor had once remarked to Anne, "That's the wee-est boy I ever seen plowing." He probably was, for he had begged to do it very early, probably because he loved horses. Anne realized the school did him little good with all his absences. After seventh grade he never returned. Stocky Thomas too was growing up with the strength of a young bull, obviously a farmer at heart, and he was able to help James more and more.

Annie Jane, an intelligent, vivacious girl, worked at the railroad station just outside the village of Creeslough. She would soon be married, thought Anne, knowing that already Willie Gallagher was after her. But it was not to be as soon as she thought.

One day just after Willie and Johnnie had returned on the train to their jobs, as Anne was settling down to tea in her kitchen, a man ran down the lane and in the door breathing heavily.

"It's Annie Jane," he gasped, "she's lying down at the station, maybe dead."

Anne froze. Not another daughter surely. She couldn't lose another. She grabbed the man's arm. "Tell me," she demanded.

"She and Frances Gallagher were riding in a sidecar on a motor bike down Duntally Bray and the brakes give out. She hit her head and now she's lying there in the station."

Anne had by now run out the door and started down the road in her slippers. Another daughter. She must reach her and keep her alive. Mindlessly she walked and ran along the mile and more to the station. Why had Annie Jane ever ridden on that sidecar? Motorbikes weren't fit for anyone, certainly not for a daughter as pink-cheeked and precious as hers.

The crowd parted to let Anne through. Annie Jane lay on a bench, very white and still. Anne knelt and put her arms around her.

"Ah, me darling, can ye hear me?" she murmured.

There was no movement. Anne lifted the piece of blanket that stanched the wound and saw an ugly deep cut on her head. Should there be a doctor? What should she do? If only John were home, he could help her.

She looked around feeling weak and helpless. "Help me get Annie Jane home," she said. "I'll take care of her."

"She shouldn't move," said Robert who had rushed there from Baxter's place. "Just leave her here, Mother, and we can take turns staying."

And so, wrapping her in blankets, Anne sat quietly watching the white face. Would she live? Would she be all right?

They kept her there for three days in the station, for fear

the move would harm her. Anne and the family waited and watched, taking food and tea to her when she was conscious.

Annie Jane went home and with the energy of irrepressible youth, her badly injured head healed completely with no help from anyone. It was a miracle from God in Anne's eyes.

But there were other things to cope with. The next blow came in 1923 when Robert, a quiet, modest, faithful son, decided to go to America to seek a new way of life. It was one of the sorrows of this tiny nation that there was simply not enough work to go around for all its sons and daughters.

And so, he had gone far away, Robert, who seemed in some ways to need her the most. How she missed him. Would she ever see him again?

To her great joy, he wrote five years later and said he was coming home for a visit. To think that Robert had saved enough money to return to the old country was marvelous indeed. America must be a very rich land.

James, eighteen, read the letter with interest. He had tried three times and failed to get a guard's (policeman) job. Thomas was old enough now to replace him on the farm with some help from Sandy. He, James, could not continue at home without work of some kind. With his meager education and the dearth of jobs in Ireland, there seemed to be none available for him.

Thus when Robert, who became Bob in the States, came home, James plied him with questions about his new life, about the people, about jobs.

"Sure, and ye need nothing, but to work hard there, James," said Robert. "I've less learning than ye had in school, and I've got plenty of work these years."

"I wish I could go, Bob, for I've no need to be here. Thomas is able to farm, he's the best o' the lot to be here."

"Ye could go, James, and find a job surely."

And so, the seed was planted. James' mind rushed along the path of possibility to that wonderful country of which he'd heard all his life.

"Mother," he said, that evening by the fire, "maybe I could go back with Robert when he goes, back to America and live there."

Anne's heart stopped for a moment. With ten children there could only be one crisis or another. But James, nineteen years old, this gangly boy towering above her, the tallest of her sons, who teased Rebecca into sharing her sweets, who always did more than his share of the work, James, going to America? It couldn't be that she'd heard right.

But he was smiling at her eagerly, waiting for her answer. There was no answer to this riddle of poverty, of where to work, of a hopeless future. America was the answer, but she didn't want to give it, not now, not now.

"Son, how could ye? We've no money."

"Robert said he'd pay my way. He has enough to give me." Another remarkable thing, that Robert had saved enough to sponsor his brother.

And so it was that three months later James set off for Dublin to get his papers. Anne paid his train fare though it broke her heart to know why he went. Traveling on the train alone for the first time, James was excited and a little frightened though he had the name of a friend with whom to stay in the city. He had never been anywhere larger than Derry, a small town compared to Dublin.

After a night at the Lafferty's, he went the next day to the Council where he had to pass a doctor's examination. He had been told to give a half-crown to the doctor, not for his health's sake which was near perfect, but because the doctor expected it and might give him a bad report if he didn't.

Next he had to demonstrate that he could read. That done, he stayed another night at the Lafferty's, traveling home the following day by train. It was a chilly autumn day. A few trees here and there had changed color, making a splash of yellow against the rich green countryside. Did he really want to leave? The excitement of the train trip was waning now as he neared home, and he could hardly wait to tell his mother about the journey and sit between Rebecca and George at the table with a dish of potatoes and salt. He hadn't had a good potato since he'd left.

A small doubt crept into his mind. In America he wouldn't see his family at all. Would he miss them? It was such a long way, much farther than Dublin.

When he reached Creeslough, it was after four and already dark. The days were nearly at their shortest. He pulled on his coat, grabbed the small suitcase that his mother kept squirreled away under her bed for who knew how long, and walked home. A young moon hung like a cradle over Muckish dimly outlining the vast bulk of the mountain. It was an unusually clear night with every star winking a welcome at him.

Striding along the road, hungry, excited to be nearly home, James burst into a song in his soft, husky voice. There seemed no other way to express his feelings that night.

He saw the light in the kitchen and ran down the lane.

James Hay (author's father) with his mother in Ireland.

Chapter 8

It was the last Christmas James would ever spend in Ireland. Now on Christmas Eve, sitting in the kitchen with all the family at home, he remembered other years, other holidays. It was always a time of expectancy with dreams in the air. Even when their stockings had hung empty, when John's hard work and Anne's management had still not left enough for so much as a gift for the smallest weanes, there was hope and excitement in this kitchen.

And they had got used to this. With a close family, a warm fire, and plenty to eat on Christmas Day, the Hays did not miss the embellishments of Christmas.

Once years before, James had got a little horse and wagon as a gift, hand-carved from wood. How he treasured it until one of the younger ones got hold of it and it was broken. Sandy was the last to have it, playing with it in spite of the wheel that had cracked in half and the horse with three legs.

James looked at his brother Willie and his pretty Yorkshire wife, Nellie, sitting snugly on his lap. (There were never enough chairs to go round.) They had come home today on the train from Derry where they lived with their tiny daughter Audrey. Nellie, her enormous blue eyes shining, always brought sparkling joy with her and a gift for everyone.

Willie rolled a cigarette meticulously, a habit he had picked up to pass the time in the trenches of France. James secretly thought it looked manly to have a cigarette dangling from one's fingers, and wished he had the courage to try.

Nellie was telling a story, Charles Dickens' *Christmas Carol*, in her low rich voice. Everyone listened.

James looked at Sandy, his youngest brother, now eleven, still thin and frail. He wished for a miracle for him, an Uncle Scrooge who could pay a sum of money to a doctor for the healing of Sandy.

This was the eve of Jesus' birth in Bethlehem, all those years ago, Jesus the Son of God. James loved the story and that small God-baby, but though it touched him profoundly, the point somehow eluded him. There was an underlying meaning, some truth that had escaped him.

Nellie was concluding, "And Tiny Tim shouted, 'A Merry Christmas to all,'" and she jumped off Willie's lap and gave them all a kiss. James liked the feel of her soft cheek and the scent of her perfume.

It was late and most of the family went off to bed, but James sat awhile with only the fire lighting the room.

"Are the ducks closed up?" asked his mother.

"Aye, they are," he said. She sat beside him briefly on the bench in the corner.

"James, ye'll be far away next year," she said.

"I will, aye," he answered.

"We'll miss ye, son, but I know ye're set on going."

He nodded. He did indeed want to go, but he didn't want to leave this place, this kitchen with the teapot on the hob and his mother quietly working and the family in and out. Once he was gone, he could never return again except as a visitor. He would never live here again, **belong** here in this small secure world. There would never be another Christmas like this one.

His mother patted his leg, then went into her bedroom off the kitchen, where John was already snoring. James heard her movements for a few moments, then the bed creaked and all was quiet.

A moment later he heard his mother's low voice, "Ye can come back, if ye don't like it," she called.

He smiled. He wouldn't be back. He had to stay once he left.

The next morning the somber reflections of the previous night faded. The Child was born, the Christ had come, uncertainty was over, joy abounded.

With all her family underfoot, Anne roasted a plump goose that John had caught and killed the day before. The goose, cooking since breakfast, had filled the kitchen with mouth-watering odors. About mid-morning Anne poured off some of the liquid from the goose into another pot, added water, salt, onion, and barley, and set it to boil merrily on the hot coals.

When the boys came in from chores outside, their noses twitched.

"Mammy's barley soup," yelled Thomas.

Anne smiled. It was a tradition to have barley soup on Christmas morning. About eleven o'clock she dished it up to a table encircled by her impatient noisy family. All her children were home, Robert was back from America, and John was at the head of the table. It was as it should be though she knew it would never happen again. Like birds, they were leaving one by one and they could not be recalled. Never again would this family be whole and together.

With the soup out of the way, she hoisted a huge pot of potatoes on to the crane to cook over the fire. Back in the pantry she had some yellow turnips which needed only to be mashed and re-heated. That and the custard for dessert were already prepared.

Nellie was busy with her plum pudding. Her daughter-in-law seemed to enjoy Christmas in this turbulent crowded household. She had brought the pudding, now a tradition also, and steamed it in a pan of water.

James, watching, remembered the first time Nellie had come at Christmas. "Nellie, are ye going to give me a big piece of pudding?" he asked, his eyes crinkling at the edges.

"Surely, James, why wouldn't I?" asked Nellie innocently.

"Well, once ye didn't, and I'll never forget it."

Nellie looked astonished. There was no fathoming a boy's mind when he was hungry. These Hays were bottomless.

"Ye asked me when I was a wee boy if I wanted the big piece. When I said nothing and laughed, ye gave it to George. I was too shy to say yes."

"Oh, James," she said smiling up at his lanky frame, "I'll give you the biggest piece of all. It may be awhile til you get some again."

"Aye, it will surely," he said soberly.

It was a day to remember, to carry along in his heart in the next lonely years. Johnnie had come home from Belfast with Kathleen, his cheerful, warm-hearted wife and baby Annie, the first grandchild named for Granny Hay. Annie Jane and the taciturn Willie Gallagher had walked home from Creeslough where they lived with their small daughter Frances. Robert was here from America, still hoping that somehow he might find a way to remain in Ireland where his heart had always been, yet knowing it wouldn't work. All were home for the first time in many years and the older ones knew it would be the last.

The kitchen was crowded and noisy as they sat by the fire that Christmas afternoon. The three baby girls were handed from lap to lap. Anne sat between James and Robert on the bench in the corner. She reached out a hand to the muscular leg on either side of her.

James smiled at her. This was his mother's grandest hour, to have her children all around her.

"That was a wil' good dinner ye made the day, Mammy," he said.

All his life James had yearned for peace, heart-peace. It was such an elusive thing, like a firefly in the July twilight under the maple tree outside. You reach and think it is there in your hand—and then it isn't at all. How long he had sought, and always the light was just beyond his grasp.

When James came to America, God Himself must have led him, for it was here that he reached out in faith, and lo, the Light was there before him, within him, all around him, wonderful warm light leading him on the path of the just that shines more and more unto the perfect day...

Bless the Lord, O my soul...

who forgiveth

all thine iniquities.

A typical Irish home with a thatched roof.

Chapter 9

There had been a crowd at the Hays that evening, neighbors who lived along the Rooskey Road, some from Creeslough, all talking, laughing, spinning yarns by the fire. Robert played his accordian and the crowded kitchen fairly vibrated as couples whirled to "Irish Washer Woman." Scores of cups of tea were served and no one wanted to leave.

The next morning it was cool and clear, March 23, 1929, Anne's birthday. The house was quiet, somber. James thought it felt like a death. This was the day he was to leave Ireland.

He found his mother in the cold cheerless sitting room, away from the family, her body shaking with sobs. He put his arms around her and held her tight. A big lump got in the way of his voice.

"Mother, I'll write ye often," he said. "And I'll be good. Don't cry."

"Ah, God help us," said Anne, her head against this tall son's heart. She had once carried him under her heart and here he stood before her ready to leave forever. She would never see him again. America, vast and cold, swallowed up people.

James drew away finally, and she reached for Robert who didn't even want to go. Why must they go?

But go they did, and Anne remained in the house with some neighbor women. The rest of the family walked to the station in Creeslough. Others joined them along the way, youngsters, neighbors, all going to see the travelers off to America.

At the station James shook hands with the large crowd, hugged his little brothers and sister, shook George's hand—now there was a brother he would miss—and turned to his father.

It couldn't be. He had never seen his strong, quiet father show emotion. But there He stood, his mouth held firmly, but tears in his eyes. Their hands gripped tightly.

"God bless ye, son," he said.

They boarded the train, James and Robert, waving at everyone, and the train left. Robert kept looking back, visibly moved, but James was excited. He was going to the land of opportunity, the country he'd always heard about, where money flowed and jobs were plentiful.

He looked at Robert and remembered that he must now call him Bob. James knew he was unhappy, longing to stay in this land of his birth, this beautiful green isle where lived everyone he loved.

"Bob, I'm glad you're going with me," he said. "Ye must have been wil' lonely when ye first went."

"Aye, surely to goodness, it was lonely," he said, his eyes kindling at the memory. "I'm glad to be having a brother with me." Bob, whose loyalty to his family was unwavering, was indeed glad to have James along.

Getting off the train at Derry, they boarded the ship and found their tiny state room low in the ship. It was steerage accommodation, and even that cost one hundred dollars per person, a phenomenal sum in those days. Bob had saved enough money in America to pay for James as well as himself, else he couldn't have gone. Bob likewise had got the money for his first trip from an aunt who lived in Philadelphia. Each immigrant helped another to this legendary land.

James, hopeful, young, and strong, gave little thought to the hardships, the loneliness. He knew he could work, and Bob said that was all that mattered.

There were eight days of rough sea before they reached

New York City, that confusing conglomeration of noise, traffic, jaded cynicism, and eternal optimism that make New York unique. James, watching from the deck, felt less confident now. The pier was a seething mass of shouting, rushing people, all going their own way with only an occasional immigrant like himself looking lost and alone.

To make matters worse, Bob with his re-entry papers was allowed to get off right away.

"I'd stay with ye, James," he said, "but Elizabeth Buchanan needs me to help her." Elizabeth was a cousin traveling first-class who depended on Bob to help her find her way.

"Aye, I know," said James. It didn't occur to either one to let Elizabeth with her greater affluence fend for herself. Bob would have to look after her and abandon James who was not allowed off the ship until the next day, if then. For all he knew, he might be detained at Ellis Island awhile.

Bob, worried and torn in his loyalty to James and his innate courtesy to his cousin, got off the ship after final instructions to James.

"Get on the train that will stop at the Broad Street Station," he said. "And mind, your money doesn't get stolen."

"I'll be careful," promised James.

"Here's ten dollars to get your ticket," he said and shaking hands, he quickly left.

There was nothing to do that night but go to bed in the lonely stateroom on the ship and wonder what the morning would bring. He knelt and said his childhood prayers. What was ahead? How would he find his way in that sea of people? Would Robert be there to meet him in Philadelphia? It was such a huge place, America. There were more people in New York City than in all of Ireland. Whatever had inspired him to come?

But like it or not, he was here to stay. There was no money to go back now.

Up at dawn the next morning, he paced the deck, waiting to leave. A Catholic priest smiled kindly at this greenhorn, telling him that everyone got settled in this nation and found work. A big strong youth like James would surely find a job and make good. It comforted James to talk to him.

Then the priest disembarked. As he walked off the gangplank, a dainty young woman accosted the priest. They spoke briefly, then the priest turned and waved at him. The young woman boarded the ship, determinedly getting past the barricade of red tape, and made her way to James who had been watching with interest.

"How are ye, James?" she said forthrightly. "I'm Maggie Smith, a friend of Bob's. I came here to meet you both, but he told me to wait for you while he went on with Elizabeth."

James sighed in relief. He shook hands with Margaret, who seemed about half his size, and was surprised at the strong grip of her hand.

It was easy then. Margaret knew her way around and talked reassuringly to him. She was only nineteen, the age of James himself, but she had already lived in the States for three years. The Hays knew her family in Garten, but James did not remember seeing her before. "Wee Maggie," as she was often called, was tough and capable, and she soon had James on the train headed for Philadelphia.

Clacking across the brown countryside touched with early green that April day in 1929, James knew this was the vastest, flattest land he had ever seen. No wonder everyone came here to live. Why, this country could absorb thousands, millions, and still have room to spare. He thought of the small crowded farms of Donegal, the rocky wasteland, the treeless, heathery hills, and knew this single fertile state of New Jersey could probably contain Ireland. What a country.

That afternoon Margaret and James arrived at the station to Bob's immense relief. He took James immediately to an Irish couple who gave him room and board in their home. Older folk, they had long since forgotten the hunger and longings of youth. While he stayed there, James seemed to be hungry always. The meals were tasty but never enough for him. Mrs.

McNeal would pass him a bowl of potatoes that he could easily have eaten by himself and left none for anyone else. Indeed the pot of praties cooked in one day at Rooskey would be a fortnight's supply here.

James quickly got a job as a gardener at Ford's estate nearby where he worked long hours. There he learned to push a lawn mower straight, to plant trees, to do neat, careful work for rich folk who had in those days money to spend on luxurious gardens and lawns.

One day Mrs. Ford asked James and his friend, Eddie Moore, to plant a hedge, perhaps one hundred feet or more. It was slow, heavy work with each bush weighted by a large ball of earth around the roots. The two men worked most of the morning making sure the good side of each bush faced the drive and the street. Mrs. Ford would surely want the best side to show to anyone driving in.

She didn't. That afternoon she came out to inspect the work.

"Why is the bad side facing the house?" she asked. "I want the hedge turned around."

James looked at Eddie who said, "Yes, Ma'am, we'll change it."

The vagaries of the rich. There was no telling ahead of time what they wanted. Slowly they went back to the beginning and began to dig up each heavy ball of earth, wrap it in burlap, turn it carefully, and replant it. The small lunch that he had eaten did little to help.

In late summer James began to look for another job, something to hold him through the winter. These gardening jobs were seasonal. Several weeks later he found one at Beaver College, stoking two furnaces to make steam for the electric plant. He had to rise before dawn and get them going, seven days a week, but it was a job, not to be underestimated in 1929.

All was going well. He had money to spend, some in the bank, and he felt rich indeed. Most of the time he worked so much that he had no time to be lonely. Except on Sundays. Then there was no family to visit, no hearth to sit by and warm his feet, no mother to listen to him, no Rebecca or Sandy to tease. On those long afternoons he would think of that kitchen at Rooskey and every lanky inch of him longed to be there even for ten minutes to see, to **see** that it was all the same, to smell the fresh scone and the turf smoke, to listen to the sound of the wind through the whin bushes, to have tea with his family once more.

When Sunday evening came, he would take himself to the Bradys. Now there was a home of laughter, light, crowds, and always a fresh pot of tea. Mary Brady was a sister of Wee Maggie. She and her family held open house for every lonely Irish immigrant who turned up on their doorstep. James loved to go there. Mary's brothers, James and Jack, were surely the best storytellers in all of Chestnut Hill, and regaled the Sunday evening crowd with accounts of escapades that could only be regarded as tall tales. How they laughed as they told them, and the listeners, near hysterics, would forget the long lonely week ahead in the warmth and liveliness of those moments.

At the Bradys' house James would fill up on bread and scone and good will. Homesickness would have to wait at the door and follow him to his room later. But by then he was tired and went to sleep as soon as he lay down in his quiet room.

In September the telegram came. It frightened him. Tearing it open, he read the stark message. "Father killed. Fell off scaffolding and struck his head." A letter followed later with the sad details.

His dad, his strong, intelligent father had fallen, crushing his head, that fine mind of his snuffed out. How could it be that a man as capable and strong and fine as his father was dead?

He remembered him at the station, shaking his hand, with the unshed tears shimmering in his eyes. How little he thought that he'd never see him again. He remembered the time he had commended him on the way he, James, had plowed, and the pride he felt as a young lad that his father had noticed. He saw him sitting in the corner of the kitchen reading, he saw him helping neighbors with plans for building a house or byre. He thought how he helped plan the Cooperative in Creeslough, the shop that served the whole area with everything from lumber to salt, the profits of it going back to its patrons, the people themselves. And he thought too of the respect that his dad had, the toil that he did unceasingly for his family.

What would his mother do? She wasn't all that old and there were still children at home. Sandy was only a boy yet, and maybe never would be well enough to work much. Thomas, of course, did the farming now, a big strong boy, and Rebecca helped her mother.

How James longed to be there now. It wasn't that he had loved his dad so deeply, for John Hay had been an austere man. But he had respected him, admired his intellect, his great strength, his humor and kindness and leadership in that small, tight-knit neighborhood. Even local Catholics had respected his father and he had been impartial in his neighborly duties toward them. The usual Catholic-Protestant animosity he had failed to pass on to his children. For his time, there had been remarkably little prejudice in John Hay.

All of this James remembered that sad September day. He wished he had loved his dad more, that he could go back to that final farewell and thank him for being his father, for giving him superb health, physical and mental, for showing him how to work hard and uncomplainingly, with inherent satisfaction in the finished job.

But it was forever too late. He wouldn't see Dad again. His shoulders shook and he wept. Would he ever see Ireland again? What if his mother died also before he got back? For the first time the immensity of the gulf between them gripped him.

Where was his father now? That there was a heaven he believed implicitly, but like Thomas of the disciples, he did not know the way. Surely a man as respected as John Hay was in heaven. Surely his goodness would outweigh any bad deeds he might have done.

But in his grief, it was small comfort. For James wasn't sure that his own good deeds were all that weighted. What if he, James, never reached that place, that abode of God? The gropings of his mind led only to more questions and darkness, and always just beyond where he could see was clear lucid light, the fresh breath of truth that would only just touch him and then recede again. If only he could find it, find **Him**, God Himself. If only he could know.

Bob came that evening and they talked somberly together. Bob wanted to go back, but neither had nearly enough money. Besides, the funeral would be long past by the time they could get there.

In the next weeks Dame Autumn with her last fling of color danced carelessly into the drab arms of November. James was amazed by the constant cold, bleak, brown countryside, so different from Ireland's eternal green. The dark early nights, hard work at the furnaces, the unforgiving frost, the persistent loneliness fell upon him like the heap of cold wet leaves that he raked at the college.

There were bright moments each week that shone like beacons to keep him going. There were Sunday evenings at Bradys and occasional Irish dances when Bob was in demand with his accordian. James liked to dance, but with his height, extra long feet, and thick muscles, he felt awkward. Undaunted, he danced anyway and enjoyed a circle of girlfriends, none of them serious, but all pretty, Irish, and friendly. He learned to smoke to fill his empty hours and gradually the winter passed.

At the end of that dreary first year, he was able to get a car, a natty 1924 Chevie, polished to within a gleaming inch of its life, and a new world opened. Gone were the days of trolley cars and time-tables. He could now ask a girl with pride to go with him for an evening, knowing that she would ride in comfort.

When spring came, the glory of it filled him with a sense of well-being. Like the trees fattening with buds and the daffodils sticking inquisitive noses up to sniff the air, James' natural optimism was surging and throbbing with expectancy. He had survived one year in America, he had a car, and he could leave this winter job and return to gardening again. Who knew what lay ahead?

Chapter 10

Fifty miles west of Philadelphia in Lancaster County lies an obscure country road going south in Beartown off Route 322. It meanders around several bends and houses, turns steep before it reaches the top of the Welsh Mountain with wonderful views of the Conestoga Valley, then goes down the south side into the Pequea Valley.

The Narvon Road, as it is still known, was in the early part of the century a dirt road. Though Narvon never merited even a pinpoint on the map, yet it was in those days a place of relative importance in the area.

For one thing there was a post office and general store midway up the hill, whose owner, proprietor, and postmaster was Harvey Whitaker. The Whitakers lived in a large rambling house with a wide veranda around three sides. At the north end of the home was the separate post office and store in which was sold all that anyone could need: groceries, dry goods, lumber. The eye-catching attraction of the store was a great brooding moose head, shot in Canada by Whitaker himself, the delight and terror of children.

Whitaker's store was the hub of the neighborhood and one went there not only to shop, but to visit with friends and to find out if Mary Kilhefner had her baby yet, or if the Solly Weavers were finished with their house yet.

The Whitakers were obviously the first family of Narvon.

But down the road a couple hundred yards lived a lesser family, Ed and Lizzie Russell and their children. From the road a lane ambled in through the woods to a clearing at the other end, probably twenty acres, with a barn square in the center and to one side a small log house. It was known as the Russell homestead, for Ed's grandfather George had first lived there, having a butcher shop from which he carried his produce to the market in Reading.

Old George had been known for his godly life and his great physical strength, both of which he passed on to his family. Once George, on his way to market early in the morning, was attacked by a man. With his enormous shoulders and arms he had seized the man and thrown him against a tree. However, when he looked at him closely, to his horrified dismay, he saw the man was dead.

He reported it immediately and stood trial. Because of the great number of witnesses attesting to his good life and since the deed had been in self-defense, he was acquitted.

Ed Russell, his grandson, was like him in his great natural strength and devout life. Married to Lizzie Hess, he lived with her in White Horse for a few years where their first child Charles was born and died six months later. From there they moved to this forsaken farm off the Narvon Road where Lizzie endured bleak loneliness and hardship for the next ten years. Her work was legion—making soap, feeding and milking cows, raising chickens, working a large vegetable garden, cooking vats of applebutter and pearbutter over an open fire outside. And every couple years another baby was born: Mary, George, Miles, Curtis, Emily, and Sadie.

Emily, the sixth child, was a round-faced, sober little girl with huge brown eyes. She loved solitude, and Lizzie often found her wandering alone through the fields or sitting in the barn near a cow. Sometimes she went too far and Lizzie's heart would lurch in fear as she thought of the woods with the mine hole full of water where a small girl could drop in and be lost forever. But when she called, Emily would appear, slowly, a sunny smile on her round face.

When Emily was four, Lizzie inherited a sum of money, enough to buy the house at the entrance of the lane on the road and leave this lonely log cabin so far removed from people.

The Russells loaded their few possessions on the wagon, making several trips in and out of the lane, and settled into the new house. There were two small rooms downstairs and two upstairs with an attic on top, a comically tall narrow house with a white picket fence around the small yard.

For Lizzie it was a mixed blessing. She was nearer people, and the sound of wagons going up and down the Narvon Road to Whitaker's store was a pleasant and sociable sound. But twice a day in all kinds of weather and seasons, she had to walk in the lane a quarter mile to the barn where she milked two or three cows by hand and took care of the chickens. On bitter mornings she would dart along like one of the chickadees, her tiny figure disappearing into the darkness of the woods and only the lantern visible, shining on the snow. When she returned an hour later, she would find her children crowded in the kitchen waiting for their fried mush with syrup or perhaps potatoes fried in lard. For Lizzie herself it was often coffee soup, as she called it, some bread dipped in coffee and milk, and eaten quickly.

Soon after the Russells moved into the new house, Ruth was born, the last of the six living children. Her childbearing finished, Lizzie's work, though hard, was manageable. A quiet, undemonstrative woman, she rarely showed any emotion other than to smile quietly or squeeze a small foot or hand.

Ed Russell loved and feared his God. Each Sunday he took his children to church where he himself would teach a Sunday school class or lead in the Wednesday prayer meeting. But in spite of his easy smile and sociability, his great inner fear was that he might not endure to the end, that he could be lost. It was a matter for much soul-searching. There was a pessimistic streak, a darkness that sometimes overwhelmed him, making him wonder if he ever could please God. The Russell heritage was to honor and fear the Lord, and this he did to the best of his knowledge, but always, always, there was the sense that one grave sin could undo it all.

Yet essentially he was a happy man. Blessed with precious few of this world's goods, he had his family, his land, and neighbors who accepted him not only as something of a religious eccentric, but a likable, hard-working friend as well.

The acts of God were inexplicable but not to be questioned. Two of his sons, Charles and Miles, had died as babies and a third was crippled. For awhile it seemed as though George would never walk, but he finally did. A tiny hunchback, he was thin, frail, sober, with big brown eyes watching the world timidly and cannily.

How he got those eyes, Ed didn't know. The Russells were blue-eyed people and Lizzie too. Yet there they were, George and Emily, with brown, penetrating eyes, especially Emily. This little girl, the prettiest in the family, had been born with her mind made up. She was independent and, for that time, unconventional. Seldom did she play with Sadie and Ruth, her younger sisters, at their dolls under the willow tree, but she would more likely be climbing the tree with Curtis or tearing around the barn, her long braids flying, screaming with laughter as she fell into a pile of hay.

Thus it was a special sorrow when Emily fell sick in bed with a severe case of rheumatic fever. Her knees and legs ached so that she would cry though she wasn't usually a crying child.

Eventually the doctor allowed her to go to school, but only if she repeated the previous grade, so there would not be too much exertion upon her.

For Emily it was embarrassing. She knew the other children thought she had failed a year. How does a child explain that she is too ill to go on to the next grade when she is fit to be in school at all? And being painfully shy as were all the small Russells, she merely tried to ignore the taunts of some of the crueler ones.

Though she recovered from the fever, the shadows of it lingered. Emily's heart and circulation were weakened and she never came into robust, full health again.

When Emily was twelve, Aunt Emma suggested that one of the children come to her and work as a servant for Mr. Roland in New Holland. Lizzie spoke to Emily and found that she was willing to go on one condition, that she not have to attend the large town school with its more worldly-wise students. Ed and Lizzie agreed since she had completed seventh grade. That was enough education for a girl. And so Emily got on the train at the Narvon Station and went to New Holland seven miles away to begin work.

There was loneliness and fear, yet excitement too, in leaving home. Though she often came home for weekends, it was that step of separation from which there is no real return. A new self-awareness and independence made it impossible to have quite the same relationship to her family. She loved them, but she had become a kind of outsider. She was set in a path apart from the others.

Yet a cloud came to settle on her, a cloud that afflicted several in her family to varying degrees. Was it a combination of Ed Russell's spiritual uncertainties and Lizzie's timidity, the two wedded together into a burden of depression that they unwittingly handed on to their children? Or was it simply an innate tendency of Emily's to doubt, to seek tangible proof for matters of the spirit?

However she received it, Emily's teen years were beset by ogres of fear. Somewhere she had heard of the unpardonable sin and the thought stayed with Emily in those New Holland years and after. What was such a sin? What if she had committed it? How would she know? Was this why she felt such uneasiness and dread at times? These were self-perpetuating questions, doubt begetting doubt, fears increasing, all magnified because of the near-sightedness of looking inward, always too shy to pull out the doubt, hold it at arm's length, and ask for a second opinion.

As time went on she came to think firmly that she had not believed and that she never could believe because of this elusive sin that escaped her, yet must be real, else why did she have such inner misery? To talk about it to her family was impossible. What shocking knowledge to give them—that she was forever lost. It would only hurt them and not help her. So she maintained a cheerful exterior and sense of humor.

A dreadful dream kept recurring in which she would find herself in a hallway. Two doors led from the hall and she would choose one, going then into a room that had a lower ceiling. From there she opened another door and went into yet a smaller hall or room. Each door of the maze led into lower quarters, but she couldn't go back for she had forgotten the way. Horror would set in as she found herself in smaller, tighter rooms, finally crawling through a tiny opening, gasping for breath, then waking suddenly to find herself at home in the small attic room which was hers now since the work at Rolands had ended with the death of Mr. Roland.

The homeplace was crowded always, and now that Emily was back again, she had volunteered to stay in the attic, not without a light however. She kept a small lamp lit by her bed, and when she awoke from the horror, trembling, released from the dream, but her soul still going through the spiritual maze, she didn't face the pitch black night at least. That light, burning steadily, was perhaps a symbol of the Light of the world after which she groped with all her heart and grasped, only to have it snuffed out by Doubt and Fear, those twin demons that lived with her.

She first heard of Bloomfield at Villanova when she visited her Cousin Emma who worked there. Filled with gardens, wide-spreading trees, marble statues, and pools of water surrounded by rose arbors, Bloomfield was the loveliest place she had ever seen.

There Cousin Emma had the care of the gardeners and chauffeurs, a dozen or more men. She cooked their meals, tasty, abundant ones, and cleaned the bedrooms, the kitchen, and the large dining room. She needed help, and when Emily came to visit, it seemed a job tailored for her with her rather uncertain health.

For Emily herself it was a relief to have a job and income again, meager though it was. The misery of nights alone in the cold cheerless attic at Narvon faded a bit in the distraction of work and the exquisite setting of this estate. She quietly fit into the routine of Cousin Emma's kitchen.

Chapter 11

The first time James saw McFaddon's estate at Villanova, he liked it. Bloomfield, as it was called, encompassed a large French-style mansion surrounded with acres of lawns, gardens, and trees. These latter took his eye first, larger than anything he had ever seen in wind-blown Donegal, with powerful trunks and low-hanging branches. There were oaks, maples, spreading elms, and exotic ones from other parts of the world, a cypress tree from Lebanon and holly bushes, thick with polished foliage from Britain. In the greenhouses were orange and lemon trees, palms from Africa, and bamboo from the Orient, along with a wide array of flowers, the likes of which he had never known.

Six men, including James, worked on the grounds, keeping up with the multitude of rose gardens and flower beds, cutting the lawn, pruning trees, painting fences, doing anything that was required to keep the place beautiful. These six gardeners ate together with the chauffeurs each day, and for once, James got enough to eat. The first day he was there, he thought he'd never had anything better than the roast beef prepared by Miss Dunlap, the cook. He was grateful for a place that seemed to be prospering in spite of the depression everywhere.

Serving their table was a tall, graceful girl in a flowing green dress. She had large brown eyes and hair that seemed to change color as she moved. One moment it was brown, dark brown, but when she stood by the window, the sun sent red streaks through it. She looked far too well-bred to be here in the servants' kitchen, but here she was.

"Who's the girl?" he asked George Mortenson, who sat next to him.

"Oh, that's Emily Russell," he said. "Pretty girl, but won't talk much. Too quiet."

James liked her name. "Where's she from?"

"Oh, up the country somewhere. Miss Dunlap, the cook, is her cousin. Emily helps her in the kitchen."

James managed to smile at Emily a few times, but he felt far too Irish and unlettered to address an American girl beyond a few words of greeting or teasing, which with his brogue she didn't seem always to understand.

But as the days went by, he found himself drawn to her. She filled his mind when he was alone. How could he meet with her? One evening looking out his window from the small room above the garage that was his, he saw her dressed up ready to go out. James drew in his breath sharply. Unaware that she was being watched, Emily walked out from the house in a beautiful yellow dress and smart shoes. She looked like a tall daffodil with slim pure lines.

She got into the driver's seat of a Chrysler and James whistled softly under his breath. She could **drive**. And what a car. Who was that old man getting into the car with her? James felt a pang of unreasonable jealousy. She was too young and pretty to be with a man that old—why he could be her father nearly.

In a moment Miss Dunlap came out and another woman, obviously the man's wife. James sighed in relief. The car drove off with Emily, shoulders back, hands gripping the wheel, driving as though it were second nature. She could really handle a car. Who was the lucky man who had taught her?

James was left with his thoughts. He had to find some way to get acquainted with this woman, to visit with her, to take her for a drive in his car.

70

A few days later as he worked in the garden, he saw them coming toward him, Emily and Isabel, a friend of hers.

He leaned on his shovel, smiled engagingly, and said, "It's a fine day the day."

"It is surely," said Isabel of Irish parents. Emily said nothing, but she smiled at him.

"Where are you girls going?" he asked.

"Just for a walk around the garden."

James plunged in. "Would you like to have a ride in my car? I could take you to Valley Forge when I'm finished here."

Both of them agreed, then continued their walk. James happily finished transplanting the tulip bulbs.

He'd done it. He would get Emily into his car. He would never have had the audacity to address her alone and ask for a date, but this way he could hope something might work out.

About six he finished work for the day. After a quick wash and change of clothes, he drove his car to the door of the kitchen. Jumping out, he opened the door of the car, but to his dismay Isabel slid in easily, leaving Emily by the window to look out. Isabel talked steadily.

He tried to draw Emily into the conversation and occasionally succeeded, her clear voice carrying easily above the noise of the motor. She looked stunning in the same golden dress she had worn when he watched her from his room. He liked the way she had of enjoying everything. She noticed the robins building the nest in the large maple by the gate, the hedge newly trimmed, the color of the sky in the west, a group of children playing in a mud puddle. It was his own sense of wonder reflected more quietly and serenely in her.

The ride lasted as long as he could make it, winding around the dogwood trees massed in pink and white bloom at the park. He bought them each an ice cream cone before he took them home, making sure he dropped Isabel off first. He **would** have a few minutes alone with Emily.

Parking by the kitchen door, he turned toward her and said

71

quickly before he lost courage, "I've enjoyed the ride, Emily. How about going to West Chester with me on Sunday? I have an uncle who lives there that I visit every wee while."

Emily paused a little. James had yet to learn that she did nothing in a hurry, and his heart sank. Though he didn't know it, she was taken off guard. She had thought all along that his real interest had been in Isabel with her Irish heritage. He surely would not want an American girl with so many pretty Irish ones around. Thus she had to adjust her thoughts a bit.

And then she said, "Well, I think that would be fine. Yes, I'll go."

And with her smile that gave her face unusual sweetness, she thanked him for the ride, stepped outside, and went into the kitchen. James went to his room astonished and strangely humbled that he had finally arranged a meeting with this American girl. Whatever would his mother think? She would prefer an Irish girl for him, he knew.

No matter. He needn't tell her. In Ireland courting was done quietly with secret meetings as long as possible til finally it was discovered. The American custom of openly dating was new to James. He liked it. It fit his forthrightness, but he was reluctant to tell his family about Emily yet.

The next weeks they had several such dates. And James talked to her every chance he got, loitering after dinner when the others had left, visiting in the evening when Miss Dunlap opened her small sitting room to them, working there on a jigsaw puzzle, anything to be near Emily.

There was a reticence about her that intrigued him. She seemed glad to be with him but there was something in the way, some hindrance that he couldn't put his finger on, some aloofness that held her back.

One evening he said, "Emily, there are some meetings over in Garret Hill that Johnny Moore told me about. He and his girl are going and wondered if we'd like to go along."

Emily smiled. "I'd like to James. I heard about them."

She seemed to be more pleased about that than going to an Irish dance or the movies. Was there a religious streak in her? Was this the key to her differentness?

At the meeting the next evening they sat with Johnny and his girl who was also an American. James had been to church all his life, but never to an evangelistic meeting. There was a fiery little Irishman, Jack Rutledge, preaching, and he had no mercy for anyone.

James sat spellbound. Never had he heard preaching like this, hard-driving, convicting, pointed, biblical. Mr. Rutledge shot off verse after verse: "Be sure your sin will find you out...the wages of sin is death...as many as received Him, to them gave He power to become sons of God." Each one went straight to James' heart. He couldn't move. He could only listen, half leaning forward, like the hart panting after the water brook, so panted his soul for God.

He had looked so long, ever since he was small, for truth, God's truth, he had yearned with all his heart to know God, to have peace in that inner man that was the real James, in the core of his being. He had even read the Bible daily these last months hoping to find what he looked for though he couldn't name it.

Was this simple gospel message the answer to the riddle, the end of the search? It had the hard ring of reality. In spite of the emotional excess, the volume, the discomfort, he knew he had struck the truth. The Word of the living God, whatever the odd-shaped vessel that carried it, was what mattered in the long run. He knew the Bible was the Word of God, but he had no idea it said things like this man quoted. He would look up all he could remember.

The invitation was the worst part of the meeting. He squirmed and hoped Mr. Rutledge wouldn't see him, his tall form towering over most of the others. He had never seen that done before, a plea for those who wanted to receive Christ to go forward. Emily stood very still beside him, her head bowed, and he had the uncomfortable feeling that she knew exactly how he felt. He rooted his feet to the floor, sang as best he could through the invitation hymn, and hung on to the seat in front of him.

It was over. That night when he kissed Emily good night, she said, "Did you like Mr. Rutledge?"

"Uh-yes, I did," he said, then added impulsively. "Shall we go tomorrow night?"

"Yes, let's," she said. "He's a good preacher, James."

And so it was that they went every night that week. Johnny and his friend soon stopped attending, but James with Emily was drawn back night after night by the plucky Irishman and his powerful preaching.

Then suddenly he decided he wouldn't go again. It was too uncomfortable and the man played on his emotions. He needed time to think and maybe to forget if possible.

But try as he might, he couldn't forget. The Irish dances, a good movie with Emily were a temporary relief, but the old haunting questions kept coming back, especially at night or early in the morning when he was alone working in the gardens. And he knew Emily was disappointed that he had stopped going. He tried to forget her too and flirted with several girls at the dance that night, but they seemed frivolous and empty. He had fallen in love with this quiet American.

And so, he knew he had to go back to the meetings. No matter how wretched he felt, he must know, **know** if what he sought was real, was true, or just a crazy restless longing that never could be satisfied. Did anyone else feel as he did?

And if he did call on Christ, what would it mean? He had never done anything half-heartedly. If he became a disciple of Jesus Christ, he would never be able to go back, of that he was sure. It had to be a commitment forever.

The old conflict resumed, that had started in Eden, the conflict of self versus God. "Choose you this day whom you will serve," thundered the preacher that night. It echoed through the night and into the next morning as he cut the grass at Bloomfield.

Choose. To think that God had given him, a mere atom in the universe, the choice. God was not forcing it upon him. He could refuse. God had humbled Himself, was **asking** him, James Hay of Rooskey, to be his friend, to follow Him. He could shut his eyes, his ears, his heart to the gentle, persistent call, yet that voice had pursued him all his life since he could remember. It was like—like the elusive scent of fresh rain on heather, something ineffably beautiful but so faint that it could only tantalize him, only hint at a whole way of life of which he knew nothing but longed to know.

He thought of all the times God had spared his life. The memory of falling into the well could still send a shiver down his back, and there was the time he had stepped into a deep hole while fishing with George. In both instances he could not remember how he got out, his own frantic scrambling and an angel of God. Once he had fallen into the "scralings," a treacherous quicksand in the bog, and George managed to drag him out. He had been terrified at the pull of that liquid mud on his legs. He remembered too when, as a wee fellow, a donkey had kicked him in the forehead, a deep ugly cut, and his mother had bandaged it and sat with him through the night lest he die.

Always God had preserved him. Was there a reason? Did God really love him, poor in spirit as he was? Because if He did, he could never disregard, never snub the most high God. If God was searching for him—and now he acknowledged humbly that He was—then the least James could do was to stop running and turn back to meet Him, the Hound of Heaven.

That morning in the middle of the green lawn at Bloomfield with no one near, he stopped the lawn mower and faced the Savior. He felt like Christian at the foot of the cross. His burden fell off, that heavy load he had carried so many years, which had only gotten heavier each day. It was gone. James straightened his shoulders and knew he was facing a whole different direction, a new life. There was an inner illumination which he was never able to explain to anyone, but which he never doubted. Old things passed away, and behold all things were wondrously new.

He looked around. The grass looked richer, greener somehow, and the rose gardens glowed with beauty. He wanted to leap and laugh for joy, like the lame man healed at the temple gate. The morning passed as a dream. He did his work, but his heart was skipping and frisking about like the rabbits that ran in and out of the hedges.

Later that same day he found Emily and told her what had happened. She smiled as he knew she would, and then a shadow crossed her face.

"You know Him too, don't you, Emily?" he asked. Surely this woman who had prayed for him and encouraged him to go to hear the gospel, surely she knew this overwhelming joy.

Emily hesitated. "James, I thought I did. I went forward in church when I was a girl, but I have so many doubts. I—I am so afraid that I am beyond His grace, that I can never know Him."

Her eyes filled with tears. "I have never told anyone how I feel. And you least of all because I wanted you to find Christ even if I can't."

It made no sense to him. His heart was singing, ringing with the joybells of Heaven, but the woman he loved, though rejoicing with him, was in despair about herself. The depths of her brown eyes grew darker, looking inward at the doubt and sin and disbelief. How could he help her?

Instinctively—or was it the Spirit of God that told him?— he knew that they must together go on hearing the Word of God. The dances and movies were in the past now, and they went, sometimes every night, to services in different churches and occasionally in tents. In the next months they heard great Bible teachers, men like Harry Ironside and Donald Barnhouse. As he had been physically hungry so much of his life, so he now longed for soul-food, to eat and be satisfied, yet always hungering for more.

The Bible that he had dutifully labored to read every night for months, three chapters in the Old Testament and three in the New, was illuminated and clear now. That first night after his conversion he read in Timothy where he had left off. Verses, once obscure, now made sense. "The grace of our Lord was exceeding abundant with faith and love...Christ Jesus came into the world to save sinners, of whom I am chief."

What beautiful words, thought James, and how gracious God was to him, the chief of sinners. All the vileness, the burden of guilt, the confusion was gone now, and in its place was this light that shone more and more unto the perfect day. It was like the dawn, his favorite hour, when he would waken, never to an alarm clock but to the sweetness of bird song and see the light in the east glimmering faintly, then growing brighter, clearer with every tree and shrub edged in gold, and finally the great burst of glory that was dayspring. His soul too had seen so long the faint hint of dawn and now the morning had come, fair beyond believing.

As the weeks passed though, the light seemed to dim a little, the joy lost some of its luster, and James wondered why. Had it been just a temporary thing after all? Was it like all things in this life, just a passing experience?

One day George Mortenson, with whom he lived, said, "You're going to meetings all the time. It's a wonder you didn't get saved."

"I did, George," said James. "Let me tell you about it."

He explained his long search and how he knew when he heard it, that this was the truth. "Then one morning when I was out on the lawn working, I felt Him near and I called on Him to save me. He did, George. He changed my whole life, my way of thinking. I enjoy things that I never did before. And He gave me eternal life."

George looked puzzled, smiled politely, then went off to tell the other men that Jim Hay had taken leave of his senses and got religion.

But for James, the old joy had flamed in his heart again. This was the secret, he discovered. Telling others this good news was the bellows that not only kindled a spark in other hearts, but made his own small fire blaze again with the gladness of God.

It was a discovery that he never forgot. From that day forward his greatest desire was to tell others the truth as he had found it.

James and Emily's wedding photograph in November 1934.

Chapter 12

The day was very like every other day that month, the sun thinly shining after a gray morning. It was November 10, 1934, the day when James and Emily were married.

For James it was the victory in a long campaign. He and Emily had dated, at first rather infrequently, then gradually more steadily for nearly three years. Being a decisive person, he had soon made up his mind that this woman was for him, that he wanted no other.

But for Emily, it had taken a longer time to decide. Her actions were deliberate, colored always by consideration of every contingency and possible complication. Emily never moved in a hurry.

"But James, I am older than you. It isn't obvious now, but as we grow older, it might become so. You might get tired of me."

James chuckled. Tired of this willowy woman in green? She was wearing his favorite dress with the gored skirt and free-flowing sleeves. He liked to hear her talk, her clear voice with its American accent.

"Emily, what does age really matter when two people love each other?" His arm was around her persuasively as they had sat that Sunday afternoon in the rose garden at Bloomfield. "God brought us together, Emily. Without you I wouldn't know Him because you kept me going to hear the gospel. I know He wants us to get married."

But Emily had another obstacle. "It's my health, James. I'm

not all that strong and probably never will be. Since that rheumatic fever, I've never had the energy and stamina I should have."

Emily felt the strength in the pressure of James' arm. This vital man with boundless ambition could not possibly understand the weariness she felt at times.

"I would hold you back, keep you from doing what you want to do," she finished.

"What I want to do is to be with you," he said soberly. "I have enough strength for the two of us, Emily. You can trust me to take care of you. I want you the way you are." And he kissed her convincingly.

"But how about your family, they want an Irish wife for you. I'm something of a misfit in all the Irish gatherings we go to."

"Only because you're the prettiest girl there," he said.

And gradually Emily's misgivings disappeared. How could she help it? James was faithful to her. Besides, this winsome son of Ireland had completely mastered her heart. She loved him. He had lifted her from the humdrum of her simple life to a new circle of friends and experiences, some intimidating for one as shy as she had been, but all of them enhancing her life.

Perhaps the greatest gift he had given her was the power of his own uncluttered faith. Though sure that she was herself abandoned by God, she had longed for him to know Christ, for no one in her right senses could wish otherwise.

But with the dawn of James' new life and the constant Bible teaching they heard, a glimmer of hope came back. Could it be she was mistaken? Was doubt the spawning of Satan himself? Was he the origin of her sense of horror, of unmitigated spiritual gloom?

God does not give the spirit of fear, but of power, and of love, and of a sound mind. To Emily wiping a mirror one day in a bedroom, certainty came as clear as her own reflection in the cleansed mirror. Her heart probing, praying, seeking, suddenly found the assurance that had escaped her so long. Her barren spirit was clothed with the garments of salvation, the robes of righteousness, as Isaiah said, like a bride adorned with her jewels, and she rejoiced greatly.

Though she was to grapple with doubts off and on for many years, she never felt the bitter despair again. It was gone.

With that, her doubts about marriage ceased also. James and she were bound together in their quest for inner peace. To give him up now was unthinkable.

And so, carefully, with measured movements, she said yes, and proceeded to the wedding, smiling at the boyish joy of James.

Wedding was a misnomer, for there were no invitations, no guests, no reception. With times as hard as they were, the ceremony was a simple private one at the home of the pastor of the Methodist Church in Bryn Mawr.

Emily wore a simple, wine-colored dress with shoes to match, which deepened the color of her red-brown hair worn in a low bun on her neck. She had an elegant sweetness which had captivated James the first time he saw her. And though she didn't say so, Emily thought he was handsomer than any man she knew with the bloom of heather on his cheeks and thick wavy brown hair.

It was not an auspicious time to begin a marriage. They had no home except their rooms at Bloomfield, and the job was rumored to be precarious. For some weeks they continued living separately with treasured private moments here and there. Then the job at Bloomfield officially ceased, the estate was given to charity, and the McFaddons, like many other rich, moved to lesser quarters.

James was out of work with no prospects for another job. It was nearly Christmas, and there was nothing to do but celebrate with Emily's family and plan the next move.

With his unhesitating resoluteness, he told Emily, "We're going to Ireland."

"We are?" she said astonished. They had no job, no home, no furniture, and they were going on a trip.

"I want you to meet my family," he said. "Now's the best time to go when I'm out of work anyway. I have some money saved, enough for a trip."

It was the kind of logic he was to use often in their life together. Cutting through the natural needs of job, home, security, he saw clearly that none of these were primary at that moment, but that ties to Ireland needed strengthening, that the loyalties of the heart and of the spirit were of greater value than any material things. He was confident that he could get a job in the spring again, and with that he would provide the home.

Thus in the meantime what better way to spend the winter months than by his mother's fireside? He longed to see her again, his mother, the homeplace, and all the family. And what a honeymoon to have with Emily, spending long days on board ship, walking into a brisk sea breeze, whiling away the afternoon in the sun on deck chairs with a blanket around their legs and tea served by the steward, watching the wake furl out behind the ship in the moonlight, going to a cozy stateroom that would be home for a week, theirs and no one else's.

So using their resources, on January 5, 1935, they boarded the *Georgic* at New York Harbor and sailed off into a misty horizon. Emily standing on the deck watching the Statue of Liberty fade into the distance, knew she was embarked on a life that she had never thought possible. She was on her way to Ireland, a country which she had always wanted to see. To think that even this dream was coming true was a measure of God's care, an amazing thing indeed.

Chapter 13

The ship took its time, a leisurely, windy, midwinter passage. While still in New York Harbor, there had been a fire in the hold, then another delay at the Boston Harbor in thick fog. Consequently they made little progress the first several days.

It mattered little to James and Emily. The splendor of the sea, at times gray and blustering, at times softly curling and blue like a sapphire; the rollicking laughter with friends whose acquaintance they made swiftly, maintaining ties by mail for years after; the fun of sorting out the courses on the menu and the cutlery to use for each; the delicious privacy of their own stateroom, they who had had no home to call theirs—all made the time pass easily. Even in the third-class quarters there was elegance: heavy linen tablecloths, stewards bowing, yet withal there was a friendly informality that made even those in first and second class go down for frequent visits. The third-class deck was simply more fun.

Ten days later the ship anchored at 3 a.m. in the harbor at Queenstown (later called Cobh) where a small tender transported those disembarking at Ireland to the dock, a few small lights gleaming in the darkness from the town. A damp wind chilled them as they went through customs in the drafty building.

"Where can we get some breakfast?" asked James of a man standing on the dock.

"Come after me," he said and stalked off, his hands folded

behind his back. Occasionally he called back a remark, unintelligible to Emily, and James would answer in words equally foreign. It was as though he had never left Ireland—all the old brogue hung on his tongue turning the vowels to music. She wondered if she would understand anyone these next months.

The man pointed his head toward a doorway, touched his cap comically when James gave him a coin, then faded off into the darkness. It was only 5 a.m.

"What does he **do**? Guide tourists like us through the middle of the night?" asked Emily.

James laughed. "Who knows? He was honored to take us to a restaurant. He'll have something to talk about the rest of the day. Ireland is full of men with little or nothing to do—that's why I went to America. Are ye serr-ving breakfast yet?" to the woman at the door.

"Aye, indeed and I am," she said, a bit sleepy-looking but amiable, and giving Emily many frankly admiring looks.

They had bacon, eggs, tea, and bread, all for two shillings. After their sleepless night and early morning walk, they were hollow and ate everything the woman gave them.

"I hope our tae enjoyed you," she said as they left. They smiled, gave her a generous tip, and walked to the train station.

That evening they arrived at Drumlish in Longford County where James' sister Mary lived with her husband John. In this land of ancient alienations, Mary had done the unforgivable. She had married a Catholic and was ostracized by most of her relatives and friends, more for the humiliation and sorrow she had brought than for any real hatred toward her.

But James remembered the old Mary, the one who laughed and sang all the time, the one who had gone to those Faith Mission meetings, the one who seemed to have a light in her eyes. He wanted to see her, and when he told Emily about her, she did too. She was both curious and immensely sorry for a sister-in-law who was no longer socially acceptable.

"Ah, James, it's good to be a-seeing you," said Mary as

James wrapped his arms about her. "I couldna think ye would stop."

"Surely I would, Mary," he said. "I couldn't forget my old sister-friend."

She tucked them into bed that night with the turf glowing in a fireplace near them, where they slept better than any night since they had started on the trip. It was so quiet and the previous thirty-six hours had been so wearying that it was the next afternoon before Mary heard them stirring.

"I looked in once or twice this morning to see if ye were all right—and ye were, so I let ye sleep on," she said cheerfully.

"But we want to visit too," said James.

"Sure and we will. Now have a cup o' tae and some sausages, but lave enough room for the goose I have roasting."

They did. James hadn't had goose since his last Christmas in Ireland six years before, and he ate til he was replete that evening.

Then he turned the conversation to that which was always first in his mind, the love of God and the miracle of salvation. He told Mary and John what had happened to him in the States and he watched the glow in Mary's warm eyes. She understands, he said to himself. Marrying outside the faith and being alienated hadn't changed that heart-hunger she had for God.

"I know, James," she said, "I know of what ye speak. I think often on those meetings I went to. I'm sure I did believe then, but I've got away from it."

"That's easy to do, Mary, but if you believed on Christ then, you became His, and He's never left you since. 'Him that cometh unto me I will in no wise cast out.' He holds **you**, Mary, you don't hold Him."

She looked wistful. "Then you don't think I've committed too great a sin for Him to forgive me, James?"

"No, Mary. God forgave me when Jesus was nailed to the cross, but we don't always accept His forgiveness. The minute we come to Him, the way is clear. He doesn't hold grudges."

They talked for hours and that night James went to bed confident that at least Mary, the outcast one, was of The Way. How like Christ to arrange this brief meeting with a sister who surely needed to be loved. Little did he know then how timely the meeting was, for when they left Mary two days later, they were never to see her again. She died shortly after childbirth several months later and the child also.

Her smiling face sent them off on the train, which took them to Creeslough. There George, Thomas, and Sandy waited at the station. They all stopped briefly at Annie Jane's house in the center of the village where her four little ones were taking turns with measles and then they went on to the house at Rooskey.

As James swung back the half-door and stepped into that wonderfully familiar kitchen, the last six lonely years fell away. It hadn't changed, not really. His mother leaned against him weeping.

"What's this, Mother? I'm here. Don't cry now. And here's Emily. I've brought you an American girl, Mother."

"Ah, Son," she said brokenly, "if only your father was here. If only he was here."

James held her, stroking her hair, til she calmed a bit. Anne was not one to live long in the past. She pulled away. There **was** Emily to look over, and tea to be got. Besides, half the neighborhood would soon be in to see the Yankees, and she must have tea for them as well.

Anne faced Emily, this American whom she feared would be too posh for the Irish Hays. Within minutes she saw that it wasn't so. Emily, her dark brown eyes smiling warmly, had moved near the fire and exclaimed over its comfort.

"What a lovely room, so cheerful," she said in delight. The family stood watching her, a little awkward those brothers. She was tall and slim, her hair braided in a style that was exceedingly becoming to her face. She looked so—so American in her green flowing dress. Emily always flowed.

"I've heard such a lot about you that I feel I know you

already," she said. "James talks about his family often and I've wanted to meet you."

How slowly she spoke and what a pretty accent, they thought.

"Ye must be starved wi' cold. Here, sit ye's by the fire while I make the tae," said Anne with more brogue than usual in the excitement.

Emily sat gratefully on the bench in the corner nearest the fireplace and stretched her hands over the glowing turf. She had been cold since she came. But though her hands and feet might be chilled, in the friendliness of this kitchen, her heart was warm. They were accepting her and that was good. She had wondered if she would fit in, if they would **like** her, if they would understand one another.

On the days following, it was as James had hoped. Family links were strengthened and he knew he had been right in choosing to come. The job and home would be there waiting in spring when they got back to America, but in the meantime he was with these dear ones again. He had left as a boy of nineteen and now returned as a man of twenty-five.

A few days later he and George were milking together in the byre. It was raining and dark, but these two were catching up on the years apart.

"George," James said finally, "God has been good to me. I wonder if ye know what He did for me."

"Aye, ye said ye were saved in one of your letters, but I don't understand. Ye were always a good boy, James. What more did ye need?"

"I still needed Christ for me personally. I heard the gospel clearly at some meetings in Philadelphia. I knew it was what I'd looked for for years, since I was a wee gahser running about here on the farm."

George nodded, his usually smiling face thoughtful. He knew what James meant. He had searched too. He pushed back his stool and looked at James.

"It's hard to explain what happened. The Bible says that

we've **all** sinned, but Jesus Christ paid the price of sin when He died. He redeemed me and all I had to do was accept His payment. I did that, George, and I never felt such joy in all my life. True joy. Not marrying Emily, not coming back to Ireland, not anything has equaled the joy and peace He has given, and I would give up everything else before Him."

His words were so sincere that George's own heart reached out in longing for something so satisfying as that.

"Aye, surely ye are contented, I can see that. I'll have to be thinking about it," he said as they walked back to the house with two buckets of frothy milk to set in the pantry.

The next day was the Creeslough Fair Day, and James and Emily walked there with Rebecca. They were late going since the two women had washed their clothes and strung them over the whin bushes to dry in the bright, but rare sunshine. However, going so late in the day gave them some interesting sights of folk returning from the Fair. One, Hughie Whorsky, came toward them with a bag slung over his shoulder that seemed strangely cantankerous.

Emily nudged James. "What **is** he carrying on his back? It looks alive."

Hughie, his cap pulled down over his eyes, came stolidly toward them, apparently indifferent to the noisy, squirming pack on his back.

"It is alive. Those are wee pigs he's bought at the Fair," said James. "How are ye, Hughie? It's a foine day the day."

"Aye, it is surely, James. How are ye, Mrs.?" he spoke to Emily.

James and Hughie chatted awhile—no one ever hurried along this road—while Rebecca and Emily laughed at the antics of those two small pigs in the sack.

Then Joe McGee went by with his donkey and creels, and Emily exclaimed over the small creature with its load daintily picking its way between the ruts. To think that she was here in Ireland walking along the Rooskey Road with the hills and fields around her, the fingers of the sea reaching between, and Muckish Mountain thrust up behind them like a great sleeping bear, listening to the quaint small talk of James and Hughie, laughing with Rebecca who had so soon become a friend—she could scarcely believe it.

And so it was each day. James and Emily cycled everywhere, to Ards to see the monastery there and the beautiful forests, to Dunfanaghay, Ballymore, Glenveagh Castle, Doe Castle, and Cashel. Emily had never been so cold as she was on the bicycle those damp winter months, but she didn't want to miss anything. At night in the chilly bed she would lie awake for hours, her feet like cold stones. James, snoring beside her, radiated heat like a furnace. In the morning he was up early and out to work with Thomas plowing the fields, excited about walking behind a horse again and watching the loam turn over, the dog following the sea gulls swooping for fat worms in the earth.

It came to an end one evening in March as the house filled with neighbors for a last visit. The kettle boiled all evening as Rebecca and Anne made fresh tea and buttered scone for each group of visitors. The next morning the last sad farewells were said, no one knew for how long, and James and Emily walked down the Rooskey Road with Sandy, George, Rebecca, and a crowd of neighbors. Thomas had taken their trunk ahead, and Anne remained behind in the house weeping for awhile, then preparing dinner. They were gone, God knew for how long, and there was great emptiness. If only her John were here reading in the corner, she would never grumble at him again.

For the second time on Anne's birthday, March 23, James left home. From the station at Creeslough he and Emily went to Derry where they stopped for dinner with Willie, Nellie, and Audrey. That evening they arrived in Belfast where Johnnie and Kathleen kept them for two days until they sailed on the *Antonia*.

It was April before the ship docked in New York Harbor, and Emily and James wearily loaded their luggage on a train. What was next? Emily wanted to see her family and talk and give them gifts, but James knew a job was his first need. They had exactly ten dollars between them.

At Downingtown Station he bought a newspaper and read the ads. Through a phone call he was able to get work at Ardmore which paid two dollars a day. Back on the train he told Emily about it.

"You can stay at your parents a few days til we get settled," he said.

"Well how about you?" she said. "Where will you stay?"

"Not at Narvon," he said smiling. "I don't mind living with my own mother a little while, but I couldn't let my wife's parents keep me. I'll go to Ardmore and find a room while I work."

"Oh, James," she said in dismay.

"It won't be for long. I'll come up on weekends and in the meantime I'll look for a place for you to stay."

It was the best they could do. However, in just three weeks James had found a better job as gardener and handyman at Bethesda School where there was a home provided for them also.

For the next couple of years they led an idyllic life. Though he worked hard, there was no pressure of schedules or bosses. James had the garden to tend, the grass to cut, occasional laundry to help with, and the fires in the winter. He ate all his meals in his garage apartment with Emily. Together they enjoyed a wide circle of friends.

In August, 1937, their first child, Maureen, was born. On a blistering hot day Emily had trod heavily about her kitchen feeding a guest. When he left, she said, "James, I believe this is my time."

At the Chestnut Hill Hospital she labored for hours. She had never been so hot and exhausted. James was excluded in a waiting room where he could only wonder what was happening and why it took so long. Close to midnight he saw her, an indignant mite, surprisingly fair-skinned, bright-eyed, inquistive.

There could be nothing else needed, he thought, for joy as he held her in his huge hands. He went to his empty home that night and slept with deep contentment.

As he sat there by the window, James remembered all the times God had healed him and those he loved, the time when Russell fell probably ten feet from the porch without great injury, all the multiple accidents and sickness of both children yet with no real harm.

He remembered the time when he, James, had met death in the hospital room, felt its cold hands touch him, before it had moved on down the corridor to another room, another bed, and he felt the healing begin...

Bless the Lord,

O my soul...

who healeth

all thy diseases.

*James Hay with his
daughter, Maureen.*

*Emily Hay
with Mauree*

Chapter 14

The morning was clear, this James knew as soon as he opened his eyes. Within seconds he was on the edge of the bed scratching himself sleepily. Then he grabbed his clothes and dressed.

Emily still slept. She worked best late in the evening and went to bed often after he did. Thus when dawn came she was still in her prime sleep. For James, this was beyond comprehension. He was ready to rise at the first light and even before.

This morning he was not so early though. Maureen had been awake in the night and he had helped to rock her to sleep again.

Now in the dawn light he stopped to watch her in the crib, the pink arms wound around her head like a frame, the mass of golden curls, the dimples in repose now, and not a blanket over her. Kicking incessantly, she just would not stay covered. At first Emily had pinned the blankets fast, but Maureen would get so angry and red-faced that they despaired of her ever sleeping. Instead James suggested they dress her warmly and forget the blankets. It had worked. He patted her, hearing the little sigh and seeing her flutter her eyelids, before she returned to sleep again.

For all his size he moved quietly. In the kitchen he sat at the table with a bowl of cereal and while the tea steeped, he read from his Bible.

The wonder of God's grace and loving-kindness still touched him. He loved to read and think of all the gifts God had given him. And this quiet morning hour was his time to pray for his family, for Emily and Maureen, for the dear ones in Ireland, for those who crossed his path. He treasured these moments of solitude.

Outside the window two rabbits sniffed the air and ate the sweet young May clover. They were likely sizing up his garden to see what would be coming in the next months. And there was a multitude of birds singing.

He closed his Bible, drank his tea, ate a piece of bread and butter and stood up. It was time to go.

Before he did though, he went upstairs—as he was to do every workday of his life—to say goodbye to Emily. She heard him and opened her eyes.

"I'm going now. Are you all right, dear?" he asked.

"Yes, I think so. It was the wee hours when I finally went back to sleep after Maureen settled."

"I hear her. Shall I bring her in?"

"Please do. I can't imagine why she's awake now."

James came in with his bouncing daughter. "Why, she's hungry," he said. "Can't you tell?"

"Not really," murmured Emily. "Look at those fat cheeks."

"Bye, Tutsie," he said and gave her a hug, reluctantly setting her on the bed. He leaned down and kissed Emily. "I don't know when I'll be home. We have a big day ahead."

Outside James jumped into his pickup, reflecting how good it was to anticipate a busy day. He was no longer employed at Bethesda School, but he had become a businessman, working for himself. All day he trimmed hedges and trees, cut grass, planted and cultivated flowers, and did any other outdoor work that struck the fancy of his clients, most of them men who paid him, but their wives whom he had to please.

With the sun coming in the back window and warming his neck, he swung happily around and into Bill's drive.

Bill was his helper. He had been so busy he had had to hire a man to help. It was a gamble, but so far, a profitable one. He made enough to cover his costs, pay Bill, and give him and Emily the best income they had had yet.

Bill climbed into the pickup, a little sleepy-looking, but cheerful.

"I guess we'll go first to Friedman's," said James. "That'll take most of the morning."

It did. Mrs. Friedman came out three times and reminded him of something he'd forgotten last time. With a wry grin at Bill, he apologized and complied with her instructions.

After Friedmans, they did three more places that warm, bright day, and it was nearly seven when he dropped off Bill.

Ah, it was good to be home, he thought, as he came in the drive. But where was Maureen? She was usually at the window waving.

As he went up the steps to the back porch, he saw her at the door with a great bandage like a sling around her arm. Whatever had happened?

"Why, Tutsie, how's my wee girl?" He picked her up gently so as not to crush the arm, and looked it over carefully.

Emily explained. "I was rinsing something in the sink and had my back to the new washing machine. Suddenly I heard a little squeak and there was Maureen standing on tiptoe stretched as far as she could go, with her arm in the clothes wringer, up to her elbow. She wasn't even crying. Not then."

"Poor wee girl," murmured James. "And you, Emily, how did you know what to do?"

"I remembered to hit the release button and free her arm. She began to cry then, and I saw her little finger had been bent back, broken, and the skin was all peeled off where it had pulled at her elbow."

"Yes, but then what did you **do**?" said James urgently.

"Well," said Emily tranquilly, "I knew I had to get her to a doctor. I didn't know where you were nor how to get you, and she was crying harder all the time. Suddenly I remembered Fred Gastrock next door. I knew he wasn't working. I called across to them, and he came and took us to the doctor."

"Will she be okay?" said James anxiously.

"Nothing is broken but her little finger, and there will likely be scars on her arm, but the doctor said she'll be all right.

And she was, healing completely in the months ahead.

That summer was a flawless one except that his hours at home were so few. James loved the exhilaration of work, the sunshine, the beauty of nature, and then the quiet end of the day at home. But this year there was the added responsibility of keeping all his customers satisfied, ones like Mrs. Friedman who had a complaint every time he went there, especially about Bill who sometimes cut corners a bit. Others, less fussy, still had to be cared for in spite of occasional rainy days and broken machinery. And after a week of soggy, humid weather, Bill had to be paid though he had done hardly any work and no money had come in.

When fall came and jobs ceased, James let Bill go for the winter and began to haul coal in his small pickup truck. It was a cold, hard year. Their savings held for a while, and he hoped to manage with that and the coal deliveries. However, his truck was simply too small to carry much at a time and the profits were scant.

The worst of it came in February. There was no money at all.

"Emily, I'm not sure what to do now. There are no orders for coal, and I can't landscape til mid-March at the earliest," said James.

Emily knew how worried he was. Providing for his family was first with James. He had to do that. His dad had never failed to do that even in poverty-ridden Ireland.

To make matters more critical, Emily was expecting in April. She was large and heavy with child, uncomfortable, tired.

"Maureen has fifty dollars in her savings account," she suggested quietly.

James shook his head. "I can't take her money," he said as he watched her in the corner reading to her dolls.

"But we can't starve either," said Emily. "And you can put it back in the bank later in the summer when business picks up again."

It was the disgrace of the thing though, to take money from his daughter, money that had been given to her by family and friends, that hurt James. He couldn't, he wouldn't do it, not even to borrow it.

But a week later he had to, and he never forgot that humiliating low point when he went to the bank and withdrew all Maureen's savings. She and Emily were in the car outside and he didn't want to meet their eyes. He had a new respect for his own father and mother who had fed eleven children.

The money was enough to tide them over until he began the early spring jobs again, cleaning up lawns, digging flower beds, working in the damp, chilly March mornings, hoping there would be no more snow to hinder him.

And then on April 6, 1940, Russell James was born, an even bigger baby than Maureen had been. First a daughter, and now a strong, healthy son, a namesake. Was there ever a grander time of year than April when daffodils bloomed and grass greened and every living creature gave birth?

And Easter when Jesus rose, that season of hope and joy. But for all James' gladness over Russell and the renewal of life, for the work that was increasing daily again, for all that, he found there was a gnawing, restless feeling inside. He seemed to have left something behind somewhere, he knew not where or what, and there was no time to search for it. The whirl of spring and summer work had begun and he worked long hours.

At least Russell was a better sleeper than Maureen had been, and James didn't have to help so much in the wee hours of the night with a restless baby. Yet the two children often exhausted Emily, and when his long days were finished outside, James would help her with laundry or dishes that had accumulated through the day.

He loved putting Maureen to bed at night, and it became a regular ritual. While Russell was peacefully sleeping in his crib, he told stories to her, Bible stories mostly. A born storyteller, James could nearly rival the Bible itself for poetic brevity. It might be the story of Zacchaeus or of Daniel in the lions' den or—and here his voice would soften and sometimes shake a bit— of Jesus dying on the cross. In the dim room Maureen's round eyes would darken with sadness and wonder.

But as happy as these moments were, they were far too brief, and James seemed to be on a treadmill of work, rushing from one job to another, six days a week, keeping his accounts in the evenings, repairing broken lawn mowers, pacifying irate customers when Bill happened to cut too close to a rose bush or failed to trim a hedge straight enough.

It wasn't that he didn't enjoy it, the hard work, the regular income, the self-assurance that his own business gave him. There was a sense of pride in having got this far, a greenhorn who came with not two shillings to rub together, now "James Hay, Landscape Gardener," as his advertisement read. Then why this wistfulness, this unease, this strange sense of something gone, missing, that had been precious above all else.

James pondered it one day that autumn as he drove again to Pottsville to haul coal, not in a small pickup this year but in a larger truck. He had bought one which could take five tons at a time. He would make it through the winter financially sound. Even the Depression was easing somewhat because of the war in Europe, a tragic solution to economic hardship.

So thought James as he drove the long, winding road home from Pottsville. There was no heat in the truck, but the day had been bright at least. Now it was late and the haggard countryside was suddenly lit by a glowing sunset which faded into the gray-browns of November, like the face of an old woman smiling briefly, then wrinkling back into repose. James loved spring, yet there was beauty even in this season, clean, stark lines of hill and valley and trees, their bare arms still blessing the earth like gaunt, mute priests.

His mind raced ahead to his family. Maureen and Russell

would be eating supper. He must get home before they were in bed. He pressed the accelerator a little harder.

Funny how he couldn't seem to feel, well, contented. He, who had always had a great contentment, now felt pressured, uncertain, skittish. He must talk to Emily when he got home. He smiled to himself. Emily certainly had no problems with restlessness. Never in a hurry, she and Maureen would read a book or look at a fuzzy caterpillar on the back porch or chat to Mrs. Gastrock who could talk endlessly and who found Emily to be what no other neighbor was, a patient listener. The day would be gone, the hours passed in contented, housewifely tasks, and suddenly Emily would find her hungry husband waiting for his dinner.

The early darkness of winter had accompanied James for the last two hours of the journey, and he gloried in the light shining through the window of his home as he rattled in the drive with his truck. Inside he caught up Maureen, who rushed to him, and set her on his shoulder. In the kitchen he found Russell in the high chair happily swallowing everything Emily put in his mouth, a beautiful smile on his face when he saw James.

Later that night as he lay in bed, he said to Emily, "Things are really going well. We have more money than last year at this time, and I'm sure we can make it through the winter. Yet I don't feel settled somehow."

Emily, sorting through the laundry basket to find her nightgown, said, "Your work seems to agree with you. Your cheeks are as pink as when I first knew you, and you eat well."

James chuckled. "Never have trouble eating. But inside, I'm, well, dissatisfied, restless." He couldn't express his feelings adequately and wished involuntarily, as he often did, for more education. He who loved words had so few at his command to use.

"Well, you seem to be away from the children a lot and they miss you."

"They do?" It was a revelation to him. He knew he missed them, but it hadn't occurred to him that he was missed also.

"Yes, Maureen talks about you often, and Russell seems to be happier in the evening when you're here."

He reflected a few minutes on that, then drifted off to sleep. Never could James stay awake when he lay down at night. But the thoughts stayed in his mind and were there when he awoke early the next morning.

In late November Jack Rutledge, the evangelist, came to town again to preach for a week of meetings at their church. James and Emily offered to keep him at their home. The three of them sat up at night after the meetings, sometimes until two in the morning talking about the Scriptures.

"James," said Jack at one of those late night sessions, "are you happy?"

"I am, yes," he said with hesitation, "but I seem to be restless too. I can't put my finger on it."

"Are you working too hard?"

James laughed. "I enjoy what I do and I'm able to work hard. At night I fall asleep immediately."

The preacher persisted. "I'm not talking about your being able to do the work. A big strong man like you has no problem doing it physically. But I mean the total absorption it requires of you, the evening hours, the bookwork, the responsibility of hired men. Has it made you lose your perspective spiritually?"

James wasn't sure, but he pondered his words in the weeks after Jack went home. Could this little preacher be on to something?

He thought often of the verse, "Seek ye first the kingdom of God and His righteousness, and all these things shall be added unto you."

The kingdom of God—had he lost sight of it? Had building up a business become the most important thing to him? Had he forgotten the urgency he felt to tell others about Christ?

One night at the supper table James talked about it to Emily. Was it God Himself that made him restless? Had he lost sight of what was most important to him?

As they talked together, it gradually came clear to him. The business was indeed too demanding, too consuming. It required his full attention, all his devotion, and there was not enough time nor energy left for what mattered most to him, his God and his family.

As he and Emily lingered at the table into the evening, James reached a conclusion in his usual decisive style. He must give up the business. Even though he saw his way clear to success, he was not willing to pay the heavy price it required.

"I'll go over to Phillip Carey's where Bob works to look for a job," said James. "I'll have work with regular hours and no responsibility when I'm home. A business is great, but for me it takes just too much time and thought. I can landscape at odd jobs here and there when we need extra income."

Then he remembered something. "I'll sell the truck, but until I do, I'll have to haul coal to make the payments on it."

So for the next several weeks he worked at Carey's by day and hauled coal in the long dark evenings. He knew it wouldn't last long, but it was exhausting while it did.

Then one cold day he came home, caught Emily in a big hug, and said, "It's sold. The truck is sold."

"I'm glad for you, James," she said. "This last month has been awfully hard for you, I know."

"Oh, well, it's over now," he said. Russell was clamoring at his legs and he stooped and lifted him high above his head while Russell squealed in delight.

Sitting with his son on his knees, he glanced at the newspaper and listened to the quaint conversation of Maureen and Emily. Emily believed that if you talked to children with sensitivity and wisdom, they responded in like manner.

James sat there half-dozing, Russell in the crook of his arm, the warmth of home thawing out his legs, the odor of stew drifting through the house.

He knew home was a gift beyond price—any money he would ever earn was a poor exchange for just one evening such as this.

The Hay family in 1940.

Emily holding Russ and Maureen holding her kitty.

Chapter 15

Though he and Emily had moved several times in their married life, it came as something of a shock to James to know they would be staying in this house less than a year, the third one in which they had lived along Center Avenue near Lafayette Hill. It was a large, comfortable one near his work and near the school to which Maureen, now in second grade, could walk each day. A mile away was the local church where James took his family each Sunday. There he taught Sunday School and sometimes led the prayer meeting on Wednesday night as well. They were well settled in the community.

Then the news came from their landlord that he was selling the house. James wondered what to do, where to go. He could not afford to buy this one.

"We've been renting all these years, Emily, but I still don't have any money to buy in this area. It's too expensive."

"Well, maybe we can rent again," she said.

"We can, but who wants to do that forever? I'd like a home of my own, a place where we can stay and not have to move every couple years."

When Emily's family heard about their soon eviction, George, her brother, wrote, "There's a house for sale here across from the Narvon Post Office just up the road. You might want to see it. It's going for $2,800."

"That's a nice house, a double house," said Emily when she

read the letter. "The railroad built it and it's big and well-built." They decided to look at it.

The next Sunday they drove the fifty miles to Lancaster County. James remembered the first time he had come to Emily's home years before, he an awkward foreigner speaking a strange dialect, and the Russells, a conservative quiet family who had never seen a real live Irishman before. Ed Russell, Emily's father, had looked askance at his cigarette (thank God, he was done with them now) and quoted verses from the Bible that made him squirm.

Driving in the lane today, they parked under the bean tree, bare now, and stepped out. All the family collected on the porch to help them in, Sadie gathering Maureen into her child-starved arms, Grandmom Lizzie taking Russell's small hand and squeezing it, the others greeting them. George was coming in the lane with some winter greens in his hand, crippled George who knew where the whippoorwills and wild geese laid their eggs and where the earliest and pinkest arbutus could be found in the spring. With three days' growth of beard, Pappy, as he was called, gave James a warm handshake.

There was no fireplace as at Rooskey, but the old wood stove in the kitchen was nearly as good. Warmth flowed over them and everyone talked at once. James saw two of Lizzie's pies on the table, made with canned blackberries from the previous summer.

After dinner they walked up the road with Ruth, George, and Curtis, leaving Sadie to play with the children. A large, brown-shingled double house with a porch across the front, it appeared to belong to the trees which surrounded it. There was about an acre of land with it, enough to satisfy James' green thumb.

It didn't take long to decide to buy it. In March, 1945, they moved to the big house at Narvon, living on the south side and renting the north half for five dollars a month. James planned to make one house out of the two sometime in the future.

As pleased as he was to own his home, the move to Narvon turned out to be harder than he anticipated. All his links with

Ireland were in Philadelphia, especially with Bob and wee Maggie, his wife. Bob never seemed to get over his longing for Ireland, and childless as he and Margaret were, he poured his affections on James and his family. It was a heartache for Bob to see them move so far away.

Thus it was no surprise that first weekend when they turned up, Margaret with a bag of cakes, scones, and fruit, Bob with his work clothes, offering to help as he did many times in the years ahead.

The next months were some of the busiest in James' life. He worked ten hours a day at New Holland Machine Company in the foundry. During the long summer evenings he papered and painted the house, dug and tended the garden, planted trees and shrubs, and helped Emily get settled in the house. Friends from Philadelphia seemed to turn up nearly every Sunday to see where they lived and to stay for tea.

Russell, small as he was when they moved, turned out to be a climber. James would find him sweating, struggling to get onto a branch or on the bars of the swing, then he would jump into James' arms. Just how could one small boy contain so much dirt? James loved him dearly. Was there any delight quite like coming home from work and seeing his son under the tree playing in the sand-pile and yelling, "Hi, Daddy, come and see my bridge!"

This quiet country home was the best place for the children in spite of his own loneliness. For he found it took time to make a niche in this Pennsylvania Dutch community. He was strange, an out-sider, and he had to prove himself to be an ordinary, normal person.

He was glad for his job at New Holland Machine Company, a small but rapidly growing plant which made hay balers and other farm equipment. James worked in the foundry ten hours daily and five on Saturday. It was heavy work, but he was in his mid-thirties, the peak of a man's strength, just past the age of Christ when He died.

James thought of that one day, how the sinless Son of God became sin for him, James, not in his old age, nor in sick weakness, but in the peak of His manhood. How difficult, how dreadful it would be to die now when he had everything to live for—and how much more Jesus must have hated death, that last great enemy.

It was in September that he began to notice some pain after he ate a big meal. Shrugging it off, he kept up his schedule, hoping to get the roof repaired and the back bedrooms papered before cold weather set in.

There it was again, the pain, this time sharper one afternoon at the foundry. It was not all that hot, but James was sweating heavily. He hoped he could make it to 5:30 and do his pouring off. The boss didn't like anyone walking out on the job.

The afternoon inched along with the pain in James' side increasing, throbbing into a cauldron of misery by the time he finally got the heavy metal poured, the sparks flying around the sweating naked torsos of each man. Maureen and Russell, watching one day, had been terrified at the inferno-like atmosphere with the sparks lighting on their father.

Today he was glad no one could see him. Never in his life had he felt such pain and it was all he could do to walk out to the van that took them home. Because gas was still rationed, the men living in his area traveled together in the back of a van.

But the ride was torment, each pothole and bump making him wince and groan aloud. There was too much noise in the relaxed crowd of men to hear him and he sat hunched over in his misery.

At home he dragged himself up to bed. It was no better lying down. He writhed and twisted, trying to ease the pain. Emily hovered over him with a hot water bottle, trying to think of some way to help.

"James, it's more than just something you ate," she said. "Let me call the doctor."

"Okay," he mumbled past caring.

The next hours blended together into a mass of pain, of whispers, of the doctor's visit and the enema he prescribed that seemed only to increase the agony, of moaning that came without

106

his will and astonished him, of the children's round eyes, dark with fear, looking at him, of Emily, confused, helpless, unable to do a single thing to ease him.

In the middle of the night the ambulance came for James. The crew carried all two hundred pounds of him down the steep stairs and into the coolness of the night where the wind felt good against his fevered face. A shot eased the pain a bit and later he slept a few hours in the hospital, St. Joseph's in Lancaster.

The surgery the next morning confirmed the diagnosis, appendicitis greatly aggravated because the appendix had ruptured, perhaps as early as when he was pouring off the molten metal at work.

"Your husband is a very sick man," said the surgeon to Emily.

She nodded unhappily, knowing she would cry if she spoke.

"He should have been here hours before he was," he said. "We nearly lost him. Another hour or two would have been too late."

"We didn't know, and the doctor thought it was some kind of blockage. He told me to give him an enema."

"An enema!" exploded the surgeon. "That could have killed him. No wonder he's so sick. We'll keep close watch on him. These next few days are critical."

They were indeed. Three days after, James hit the lowest point of all. The infection had spread through his body, and though he was taking large doses of penicillin, he got weaker as the day progressed.

The children were with Granny Russell and Aunt Sadie, so Emily stayed all day at the hospital. When visiting hours were nearly over, James whispered, "Emily, I don't think I'll make it. Stay with me."

Her deep brown eyes looked into his and he saw the fear. "I'll stay, James."

He couldn't believe it. Was it to end like this? To drift off like a shadow, like the grass withering and the flower fading—could this be he? He felt astonishment and a great sense of sorrow, not fear, but sorrow, that so much was undone. The mortgage—how could Emily ever handle that? She had no strength to hold a job. And his children, he didn't want to leave them, not yet, not yet. He loved them more than himself. How could he leave Emily and the children?

He would see Jesus, of that he was certain, but he wanted to see his family just awhile longer. Too tired to pray, he lay there through the long hours of the night getting weaker.

Emily sat still by him, holding his hand and occasionally smoothing back his hair, that thick wavy hair that she loved. She was beyond crying now, just a sense of numb unreality covering her like a gray garment. This couldn't be happening.

He had gone to sleep—or was he dead? She leaned over and felt his breath. Not yet, thank God. She leaned back into her chair, a feeling of great weariness upon her, but unable to sleep. If James were leaving, Emily wanted to see him off. She would not sleep.

She thought of the death-angel passing by in the night and shuddered. The hospital had grown chilly, and there was a deep quietness. Walking to the door, she heard a nurse rustle by in her starched dress. No death-angel that. Perhaps he had passed already by and touched one here and there beckoning them to follow.

As she turned back to the bed, she saw that James was awake. Leaning over him, she touched his face with her cool hand.

"I'll be all right," he whispered. Could it be so? Was the crisis over? He drifted off to sleep again while Emily sat and wondered, at last dozing briefly herself.

In the morning the doctor came and confirmed the change, amazed at the abrupt improvement. The intravenous could be withdrawn, and James could begin to take food and medicine by mouth now. With his usual gusto he clamored for food.

"No, you may have only ginger ale and Jello," said the nurse firmly.

"But, I'm hungry, starved for a potato or a piece of meat," he said, his voice weak but just as firmly.

"You've been terribly sick," she said, "and doctor's orders are for liquids only."

James groaned. "They'll kill me with hunger," he said ruefully to Emily when she came later that day.

It was good to hear him. When James was hungry, Emily knew he was getting well.

That evening a tray with a steak, some green beans, and mashed potatoes turned up.

"Ah, I can eat now," said James.

He was just started, with Emily buttering his bread and cutting his meat. She listened happily to his jaw snap in that characteristic way he had as he ate. The nurse rushed in.

"You have the wrong tray," she said as though it were his fault.

"Did I? I've enjoyed it well," he said, a boyish grin on his face.

She snapped what was left away from him. "Here, I'll take it," and whisking out of the room, she returned with the Jello and Seven-up.

Emily was worried. "Maybe that food will hurt you, James. We should have thought before you ate, and asked the nurse."

"Not a bit of it. I was hungry. When a man is hungry, he's on the mend. You can't get well if you don't eat."

It was another of his unorthodox ideas, but as always, it worked for him. What might have killed another person seemed to give him strength. All his life he was to believe that food (potatoes and tea in particular) would cure all ills.

When he left the hospital, James missed the next eight weeks of work and marveled at his weakness. Would he **ever** feel himself again? Could he handle the heavy work at the foundry?

When the time came, he was able. And in the meantime he had the only non-working vacation of his life, the hazy autumn days passing by like golden coins on a chain. Each one was a gift from God. He helped Emily wash, hanging clothes in the warm sun, running to bring them in before soot fell from the steam engine train meandering by on the crooked rails that led up to the clay mine in the woods nearby. He played with Russell under the maple tree, pushing the small trucks around sandy roads. They went on long walks together. He welcomed Maureen home from school each day. He cleaned the attic where he found the cause of the rumblings in the wall—flying squirrels had moved in for the winter as they were to do every year. After traps failed to quell them, he decided the house was big enough to hold both the Hays and a family of resident squirrels.

October could nearly be called the most beautiful month of the year, he thought, as the green turned to gold and the sky was bluer than he'd ever remembered it. Standing outside early one morning, James said reverently, "Who could make even one day? Thank you, Lord, for this one."

His loving-kindness, O how great, thought James as he prayed. How he wanted others to know the loving-kindness of God to him, though he could never express it as he should, unlettered as he was.

And His mercies were new every morning, mercies of health and hard work with strength provided to do it, mercies to his wife and children, to his dear ones in Ireland...

Bless the Lord,

O my soul...

who crowneth thee

with loving-kindness

and tender mercies.

James Hay with Maureen and Russell in the snow.

Chapter 16

No one had ever told James just how **busy** he would be working fifty-five hours a week, maintaining and improving the house, and raising a family. A couple years after moving to Narvon, their renters moved away, leaving fourteen rooms, two attics, and two cellars for the Hays. In the next years James remodeled it into one large house which accommodated anyone who happened to turn up on the doorstep. Housekeeping was not Emily's strong point, what with her placid slowness, but in spite of untidiness and confusion, there always seemed to be visitors on a weekend. Like birds to a cherry tree in June, people flew to the old comfortable, brown-shingled house on the Narvon hill.

In the prime of life, James loved it all. Work at New Holland was tedious and heavy, but he never forgot his brush with death in the hospital. Being able to work was a privilege, a gift from God.

It was especially rewarding if a man had a family such as he had. Coming home one evening in late May, he saw Russell as usual under the big maple tree by the drive. He had been there ever since school was over, James knew, playing in the sandpile with his toys. Frequent bubbles from his wad of bubble gum exploding in his face made the dirt and sand stick even tighter.

"How's my gahser?" said James as he got out of his Chevie recently purchased when the war was over, and both cars and gas were easier to get.

"Okay. Say, Daddy, can we go swimming in the mine hole?"

"Swimming? It'll be too cold. That water is spring water and in the shade most of the day."

Maureen ran out from the house looking suspiciously dirty too.

"See, Daddy, how dirty we are," she said gleefully. "We knew you'd take us if we were dirty enough. Then we won't make such a mess in the house."

James smiled. He couldn't refuse these two sprites even if he was tired.

"All right. Is supper ready, Emily?" he called, knowing it probably wasn't. "I'm taking these two to the mine hole."

And they went, the youngsters scampering ahead with Barry dog across the field to the water that had filled up an old iron ore mine. It was treacherously deep except at the north end where one could wade in for some distance before it dropped off into infinity. Its merits were privacy, availability, cheapness.

Russell was already wading in when James caught up with them, and Maureen was squealing over the cold as she dipped in her toes. But in minutes the two were swimming and yelling to James to join them.

He shook his head and laughed at their antics. Kids, they never minded the cold water. He dipped his feet in to cool off and tried to forget he was hungry. I wonder what Emily has for supper, he thought sleepily. I'd sure like to sleep for a few minutes. He leaned against a tree and perhaps dozed a little. At least he jumped when he heard Maureen yell, then decided it was time to leave.

"Come on, you two, it's suppertime."

"Aw, can't we stay a little longer? Huh, Daddy? We just got here. Please can we come back tomorow night? Why didn't you get in? It was fun, Daddy. Don't you like to swim anymore?"

Shivering in the air, they dried themselves, then ran back the quarter mile or so to the house. When James got there, the supper was nearly ready. He set the table, poured water, and filled his plate with poundies, as they called them in Ireland.

Ireland—it was so long since he'd been there. The years, such busy ones, had flown by like leaves on a windy day, and there had never been either time or money to go.

"Any mail?" he asked Emily.

"Oh, yes," she said, "there's a letter from Rebecca and one from Mother, I believe."

He read his mother's first. "Thomas will be cutting turf soon. He has the praties planted and I walk down every day to see them. Katy's new wane is wee Thomas. That's five for them now, it's time they stopped."

Only his mother would have the audacity to say that when she had had eleven. And the wisdom—she knew how much lay ahead in raising children. How he longed to see them all and her in particular.

The years had flown. He must go to Ireland again, this time with his family. Urgency seized him, and he talked it over with Emily in the next weeks. She agreed. They must return. And so for the next two years he saved money as regularly as he could. Maureen and Russell grew enthusiastic and offered their small savings accounts gladly.

At the end of May, 1951, the four of them set sail from New York City, Pier 81, on the *M.V. Georgic*, the same ship that Emily and James had traveled on sixteen years earlier. Then it had been a luxury liner becoming a troop ship during the war. It was now a passenger ship again, lacking some of its former grandeur but having one advantage. This time there was one class, instead of three, which meant the Hays, with all the other passengers, could have the run of the whole ship, not just part of it.

James and Emily harked back to their honeymoon trip, but there was an added dimension of joy, as well as responsibility, having their children with them. Arriving at Cobh in southern Ireland eight days later, they disembarked and found George waiting for them, with a car he had purchased for the occasion with James' help.

The tiny car with the right-hand drive was a new experience for James. The five of them squeezed into it, placed some luggage in the "boot," the rest on top, and prayed it wouldn't rain. It didn't, in itself a small miracle.

James and George sat in front, sharing the driving and talking about the Lord. George had come to Christ partly as a result of James' witness and was longing to tell him about it face to face. Emily, swaying in the back seat around endless curves, would say occasionally, "James, don't forget to drive on the left side." Once he did forget altogether, and the oncoming astonished driver was forced to keep to the wrong side of the road. James and George scarcely noticed.

About eleven that night (still driving without headlights in the long northern dusk), they stopped to see Sandy in the hospital at Castlereagh. Sandy's health had declined abruptly in the last year, and though he rallied again for a time, this was James' last summer to see his youngest brother. His warm, brown eyes, so like Bob's, smiled happpily at James and his family as they waved goodbye.

On through the night they drove with only a few hours of darkness. The car was too crowded for sleep and there was so much to see. They reached Donegal and began to see familiar places, Letterkenny, Barnesmore Gap, Kilmacrennan. They hurtled along through the hills and glens, looking for fairies in the mist of the morning, past George's own place at the old Baxter farm, then turning in the Rooskey Road. It hadn't improved a bit and scarcely ever saw a car. They bumped along past each small farm. Ah, there was Whorsky's, the next was home. Down the narrow lane they drove and stopped by that dear familiar house. It was 6:30 a.m., when no Irishman was up except, yes, there was Thomas, standing like a big bear by the half door.

"How are ye's all?" he said, his huge hand gripping each one.

"Thomas, it's good to see ye," said James as he faced this brother who looked most like him.

116

Katy, wife of Thomas and mother of six now (they had evidently not heeded Anne's opinions), cheerfully welcomed them to that old, much-loved kitchen. She had moved into the homeplace, populated it with babies, and become the core of the home, much as Anne had been. She was warm and loving and sometimes as excitable as a hen scurrying after her chicks. The kitchen was soon in a whirl of activity as Katy flew about making tea, slicing bread, fixing bacon and sausages. Everyone gathered around the ample table.

Anne herself, after the first greeting, sat and cried. James put his arms around her.

"I stood outside at three this morning," she said, "and heard nothing and I feared ye weren't coming."

"We did, Mother, we're all here. Sit and talk to me."

With six-month-old Kathleen cooing on her lap, she sat by the fire with James and cast admiring looks at her new grandson, Russell, in his smart American suit.

"Mother, I can't believe you've changed so little in sixteen years," said James.

"On wi' you," said Anne. "It's you who haven't changed. Ye have two fine weanes, James, ye and Emily. I thought I would never see your children, but here ye are. I don't know how ye did it, James."

"I hardly know myself. The Lord helped us, Mother. We saved for a couple years, all of us, and the shop where I work was willing to let me go for the summer. To come for a shorter time was hardly worthwhile. I hope we'll not be too big a burden here."

"Surely ye won't. Ye'll be helping Thomas plenty—he's much busier since he has the other farm—and here in the house, we can all help. It's a wee bit crowded, but since Thomas built the two extra rooms, it's not as it was when ye were wee." She smiled in memory. "I can still see ye trailing up the stairs wi' George to bed. Come and see the new bedrooms."

117

She led him proudly to the new addition after setting Kathleen in her cradle. Anne's life now focused on this new family, Thomas' children, whom she loved as her own.

For the next two months James and his family lived at the Rooskey farm. The barley fields tassled, the rickled turf dried, the hills grew pink with heather. Every day at noon they ate new potatoes cooked with their skins on, peeled, and dipped in salt. They visited everyone James knew and loved.

How wonderful to have his family there with him, his own children finding their roots in this ancient land.

He was glad they had come.

Chapter 17

As the years went by, James had never lost sight of that first joy he felt years before when he witnessed to someone about Christ. Though he had no education, no training, no special talents, though he was just a factory laborer, he knew he must **tell** others what Christ had done for him. Never could he forget that urgent constraint, the love of Christ that had saved him and now made him an ambassador of the King. To think that the living God would use his feeble tongue to tell another of His love was beyond his comprehension but not his belief.

It was the driving force in his life. Others could preach, teach, found colleges, counsel—but James could witness. That he had probably the hardest job of all did not occur to him. But he did know that of all places to witness, the hardest was at work.

They were a robust, good-natured lot, most of them at the foundry, but that made it none the easier. There was one other believer, a precise, old-maidish man yet sincere and courageous. Together he and James had a short street meeting one Saturday afternoon in New Holland, a respectable, complacent town. Not many stopped to listen.

The next Monday at work Luke Harmon said to James, "Hey, Jim, where'd you get that sunburn? Been sunbathin'?"

The other guys laughed appreciatively. "I heard him and Earl singin' hymns, Luke. They're pretty good preacher boys, they are." More laughter.

James smiled without rancor. He understood how amusing it must seem to have him, a man who rubbed shoulders with them every day, who poured off molten iron, who sweat and got tired, to have such an ordinary man tell them about what the Bible said. That was for preachers, they thought.

Which was precisely the problem. Men like these thought religion was just for women and maybe a few men in the church, certainly not for tough-talking, muscled men as they. He wanted them—**how** he wanted them—to know that Jesus Christ was for every man, that He would come and abide with them in their hard-working, uneventful lives and color the grayness of their lives with the gold of eternity.

He was happily surprised when his boss, Rocky, came to him one day near Christmas. "Jim, how would you like to speak to the guys at the Christmas party? You know, uh, maybe preach a little sermon or say a little prayer. I think we could stand some religion."

James was both excited and nervous. It was as though God had given him a pulpit, the top of a hay baler as it were, the kind he could handle talking to men who were as unlettered as he was. But he knew too that he would be saying publicly, 'I am a Christian. This is the most important thing in life to me.' He would have to live up to that.

When the time came, there was a curious crowd of men to listen. He noticed from the corner of his eye that two of them, Butch and Reynolds, left and went over to the corner to play cards. The open mockery on their faces made him squirm. Be not afraid of men's faces, God said to Jeremiah, but it was hard not to be.

He spoke briefly. "Fellows, I'm not very good at saying this, but I want to tell you how I was saved. As you know, I grew up in Ireland and came here in 1929. The Lord Himself got hold of me through some meetings in Philadelphia and I heard there that all have sinned and come short of the glory of God. I thought I was pretty good, but God says all men are sinners. Then I heard that the wages of sin is death, but the Gift of God is eternal life through Jesus Christ our Lord. Jesus is God's Christmas Gift to me, to you.

"One day as I was working outside, cutting grass, I accepted that Gift, Jesus Christ, and He became my Savior. I was a new creature, all things became new, and I want others, **you**, to know about this wonderful joy and peace you can have by trusting Him. If you'd like to talk about this further, I'll be glad to help you. I pray for you. Thanks for listening today."

It was over. He turned to the boss and talked briefly to him, watching the men as they dispersed. "Thanks, Rocky, for giving me the chance to talk to them. I appreciate that. Merry Christmas."

Rocky nodded. "Thanks, Jim. Uh, I liked what you said." And with that he walked to his office.

It was not the only time he was able to witness to men at work, yet withal he wondered if he had any influence at all. One day the boss took his job, an especially hard one, and gave it to Butch, one of the two who had refused to listen to his testimony. At lunchtime Butch cornered him.

"You hypocrite," he spat out the words with venom interspersed with several obscenities. "Why'd you tell the boss to give me that job? You sound so good and religious and then you play up to him to give me work you don't want."

James was first astonished, then angry. "Look, Butch, you can keep quiet about that," he said. "You know I had nothing to do with it. He made up his own mind. If you wanta fight about it, that's okay with me."

He walked away and left Butch muttering to the other guys. I've ruined it, he thought miserably a few minutes later when he cooled off. I've ruined what I tried to tell them earlier.

The next two days he tried to forget it, but it haunted him. He remembered the words of Jesus, "Love your enemies, do good to them that despitefully use you."

Butch was an enemy now. It was up to James to love him and show that he did, even if it meant humiliation.

121

That third day he managed to get Butch alone. "Butch, I've come to apologize. I'm sorry I got so upset the other day. I really didn't use any influence on the boss, but I can see why you thought I did. I'd like to be friends and not have this bad feeling between us."

It was hard to say though he felt relief even as he said it. But Butch looked at him blankly, then scowled, and walked away without a reply.

James felt a sense of failure. Had he destroyed all his witness? How could God use him? He was too weak, too stumbling, too—foolish. Some words he'd read recently floated through his mind. "But God hath chosen the foolish things of the world to confound the wise...and things which are despised hath God chosen..."

He knew both Butch and Reynolds, his buddy, despised him. Luke Harmon and Les Weiler tolerated him with good-natured laughter. Some of the more serious guys respected what he said, but the majority passed by without comment. He longed to draw them to Christ.

It was years later when the foundry had been replaced with a large assembly plant and James, working on the line, heard about Reynolds.

"He dropped dead at home," said Bill who was lying beneath a baler fastening the knotter in place.

"He did?" said James nearly speechless. Why, that was the last of those four who had either rejected angrily or mocked at the gospel. Each of them, Butch, Luke, Les, Reynolds, had died an untimely, sudden death. "He that being often reproved hardeneth his neck shall suddenly be destroyed and that without remedy." It was with a kind of terror that he realized the truth of this. These were men whom he had once known well, had worked and lived with ten hours of each day for years. To some he had been, as Paul said, a savor of life; to these four perhaps, and he drew back trembling from the thought, perhaps he had been a savor of death. Had they ever found forgiveness for sin? He did not know.

*   *   *

By this time, James was busy in the visitation program at Calvary Independent Church in Lancaster. Though the church was twenty miles away, it had not been a hard decision for him to go there.

Years earlier he had first heard Frank Torrey preach at the Old Mill Bible Conference. He still remembered that message. The man taught the Scriptures, not with clever outlines and correct homilectics as the typical conference speaker did, but with profound, poetic truth that made Christ increase and all else decrease. When James heard he was from Lancaster, he visited the church soon after he moved to Narvon. As soon as gas was available again, he took his family regularly.

Under the teaching of Dr. Torrey, he felt himself growing, stretched in his walk with God. He came to know and respect men like Herb Palm, Ben Groff, Walter Rohrer, with whom he later served on the elder board.

There he also developed a friendship with Dewey McConaghay, a man under orders. Dewey's chief burden as a youth pastor at Calvary was to reach out and witness. When James crossed his path, a friendship grew that strengthened over the years as these two became fishers of men together.

Dewey gave training in how to go to a home and witness. James had done it for years on his own, but never in a perfectly strange home. Always he had gone to men at work or to his neighbors.

The first Tuesday night he went out on a cold call with Abe Snavely, a New Holland businessman who was an experienced witness. Though James was nervous, he knew Abe would be polished and relaxed.

He heard Abe say, "Uh, we've come to, uh, talk to you this evening because we, uh, want to tell you some, uh, good news."

Abe stumbled too, this man whom James admired deeply. It came as a surprise to him that even with experience, personal witnessing never was easy. There was a tension, a terrible sense of inadequacy, a conflict, the fear of men's faces that hovered over every house as one knocked on a door. It was a direct challenge to Satan and required the armor of God.

To make matters harder, the next week Abe wasn't there, and James was in command, going with a man who had never witnessed before.

But with a flash of insight, he suddenly realized that the listeners, the ones to whom he witnessed, were even more frightened than he was. The Holy Spirit **lived** in him, James, and His Presence sensed by these strangers was far more terrifying than having a door banged in one's face or a mocking look.

And so, he kept visiting week by week, remembering that he was doing it for One who had done so much for him.

*   *   *

Since the time Maureen and Russell began first grade, James and Emily were deeply interested in their children's school. Emily visited their classrooms several times and kept in touch with teachers, some of whom she respected highly.

From Narvon the children attended a one-room school, later going to a larger one in Churchtown. It occurred to James, who remembered his own brief education, that there should be some religious instruction taught in the area schools, not of a particular denomination, but simple Bible stories, the Word of God. He decided one evening to go to a local school board meeting in Churchtown and inquire about the possibility.

Caernarvon Township school board members were elected locally to direct half a dozen one-room schools as well as the one in Churchtown. That was a day of strictly local control with an annual disinterested visit or two from someone at the county office.

James liked Dan Esh, the president of the board, an Amishman whose eyes, peering out from under his black-brimmed hat, were bright, penetrating, and very wise.

"Dan, do you suppose we could have a Child Evangelism teacher come to our schools and teach the children something from the Bible for half an hour each week?"

Dan looked thoughtful. "I agree, we need some Bible teaching in our schools," he said. "Let us think about it a little while."

The meeting progressed with other business and James thought it was simply a nice way of ignoring him. But near the end, Dan brought up the subject of a half hour of religious instruction each week. The other members looked at each other, saw no reason to demur—each one privately thought a little religion was a good thing for children—and passed the measure unanimously.

James was jubilant. Each child in Caernarvon Township would hear the Word of God weekly from a Bible teacher brought in for the occasion.

It was some while later that he saw Dan again. "How would you like to be on the board?" asked Dan. "We need a man to fill out someone's term. Jake Weaver recommended you, said you'd do a good job." His sharp eyes looked up at James' height appraisingly. "I believe you could do it."

As an outsider, a foreigner, it had never occurred to James that such a job would be available to him in this close community. "Well, I've never had much interest in politics. I don't know, Dan, if I'm interested or not."

"For now, we just need you to fill out the term. You can decide later if you want to run on the ticket."

"All right, I'm willing." He knew the board had a history of quarreling and dissension. One member had even quit in anger. Did he really want to get tangled in that more than a short time? Yet Maureen and Russell were in school here. He should contribute in some way to the community.

At the first meeting he asked Dan, "Did you ever have prayer before you began?"

"No, we never did," said Dan. "We need a preacher for that and hardly ever is one here."

125

"I'm no preacher, but I can pray," said James. "I think we ought to have prayer. Things might go better."

"All right with me. You pray, Jim," he said. The other men on the board accepted it and the small audience as well. From that night on, James always led in prayer at Dan's request.

And from that night on there was never any more virulent dissension or bitterness in spite of the vast changes in the school system that were being laboriously worked out in the next years. James did run and win the next election and was on the board ten years, the last time because he was drafted and won in a landslide. Emily's meticulous records and accounts won special notice from the county commissioner when the books were checked, this in the day before calculators and computers were used.

As time went on, members changed. One year when the annual letter came from Katherine Hershey asking for permission to return to the schools to teach Bible again, there arose Bruce Trumball, who, like the Pharoah that knew not Joseph, wondered who Katherine was and if these Bible classes should be continued again.

"I think we need to think through this carefully," he said. "I know the county office does not look kindly on these classes." Bruce was always in the mainstream of popular thought, a man who made sure his influence was felt.

James was exasperated, but mindful of the prayer he had made aloud asking for harmony and understanding in doing God's will, he did not speak.

"Let's table the letter for now," suggested another.

"Fine," said Dan, a peacemaker. He did not want to quarrel with one as strong-minded as Bruce and this seemed an easy solution.

The meeting moved along. Bruce had a rather glazed look, and he finally whispered to James, "I'm not feeling well. I'm going home early."

"Okay, Bruce, hope you'll soon be better," said James. He

126

leaned over to Dan and told him quietly. The audience tonight was not very many, and they too began to go after they had given their requests and complaints.

It was late. James thought of his 5 a.m. rising time in the morning and hoped he could get to bed soon.

"Any more business?" asked Dan.

"Oh, we forgot about that letter," said Percy. "We have to give Katherine Hershey an answer about the Bible classes."

"I think it should be yes," said Dan. "Those teachers have taught nothing but good in the classes."

The men looked at each other and nodded. There was no dissenting vote.

"Jim, you're the secretary. Write to her and tell her we'll have them again this year."

"Okay," he said. And the meeting was dismissed.

As he drove the few miles home, James thought about the meeting. "I might have known You'd work it out, Lord," he thought. "They're your classes, not mine, and You can take care of them as long as You want them in the schools."

Then he smiled to himself. He hoped Bruce felt better by tomorrow.

Chapter 18

The postmark was Dayton, Tennessee, so James knew the letter was from Maureen. He loved reading her letters, full of stories of friends, classes, chapel messages, and more recently of her new boyfriend. As James sat by the table, waiting for Emily to pour off the potatoes and make gravy, his mind flew back to that grim night before she left for college.

They had read the Bible together as a family that night as they usually did, and then he had tried to pray. But his voice wouldn't stay level. It wobbled like a bicycle out of control, and he had to stop, sobs shaking him.

It was more than simple grief over his daughter leaving for college the next day. It was the knowledge that this was the end of childhood for her, that she would leave home and not return, ever again, never the same. Back for holidays and vacations, true, but it would be temporary, as a visitor, and she would be perched ready to fly again, not nestling in to stay.

He had done it far more irrevocably than Maureen did when he had left Ireland. But then he was nineteen and a man. She was only a girl, sweet-faced and so young, newly seventeen. How was it that she was going so soon? It was just a few days ago that he had brought her home from the hospital in Emily's arms. He remembered his mother's tears when he left Ireland years before, and for the first time he fully understood them. The love of all the years, the weight of it, was nearly more than he could bear that night.

Yet she had gone to Bryan, and though it was a small college, inconsequential and poor in worldly assets, she had grown and been stretched there. He remembered when her roommate, Alice McLeod, came home with her for spring vacation, Alice, whose face, like Moses, shone with the reflection of God. He had never met anyone quite like Alice, nor had Maureen, and he knew that a friend who made Jesus more real was rare indeed.

All of this flashed through his mind as he sat there unfolding the letter with the familiar peacock blue ink that had come today. It had been a good investment, sending Maureen to Bryan, in spite of the financial crunch which it caused.

He read the letter. "Last Sunday Walt and I went to church together. It was a drippy wet night and we had a big umbrella. And guess what? He asked me to marry him! And oh, I am so happy. Seems as though it can't be true. I know I'll have to talk to you to really convince you that I know my own mind…"

His hand was shaking and he cleared his throat a couple times. Marrying Walt? And her barely twenty years old?

Russell sat down opposite him. "What do you think, Dad?"

"Aargh, um well, I don't know."

"Well, I don't like it. Knotty's not ready to be married yet." Knothead was Russell's name for his sister and conveyed deep affection.

"I don't think so either. I'm not sure Walt is the one. But we may not persuade her of that. What do you think, Emily?"

Carefully setting the gravy bowl on the table, gravy perfectly smooth and as brown as the fallen oak leaves, she said, "I don't like the idea. Something's not right. It's too quick. She's got pushed into this and she's not ready for it, not really. Something's not right about the tone of that letter." Emily's perceptions were often right.

"Yes, it's false somehow. She wants to please him when he should be trying to please her. She said in her last letter that she feels sorry for him. You can't marry someone for that reason."

They talked about it all through the meal, then Russell said, "I need to apply to a college soon too. Graduation isn't too far off.

James looked at his son, taller than he was now, and lean as a flagpole, his deep blue eyes wide-spaced, his face serious. He had it to do over again, send another, the last one, away. What was happening? One planning to marry, another to leave to go to college.

He thought of all the busy years, his long hours at work each day, his evenings taken up with the school and church boards. Somehow he had not seen his children all that much. And now the years were gone and here he was talking to Russell about where he should apply for college and thinking how to write Maureen discreetly and wisely about her unofficial engagement. It had happened so quickly.

James was not one to live with regrets and might-have-beens, but if he could have changed one thing that night, it would have been the amount of time he had spent with his children. He guessed he was not alone in this. Perhaps one of the weaknesses of the church was the demands it made, the constant call to serve God, to attend meetings, to be busy, frantically so, with not enough time left for family. A living, loving example in a home was the greatest service (and perhaps the hardest one) one could offer to God.

Now in retrospect, the most precious moments of his life were those he had spent here in this home with those he loved, the times when he told stories to the children, when they all gathered under the maple tree outside and ate ice cream after the lawn was cut, when Bob and wee Maggie were here for tea on a Sunday afternoon, when the family sat around the supper table and laughed over Russell's wry tales of school, when they read the Bible together at night.

The real spiritual growth of his family had come not from his being an elder at church, but from their lives, his and Emily's, at home, their kindness, firmness, daily prayers, bedtime stories, and laughter.

Later that night he wrote Maureen in his usual happy disregard for punctuation and sentence construction. "I hardly

131

know if I can call you wee Tutsie anymore or not, your last letter was a rather sudden should I say shock, something that we didn't expect so soon. We sure hope you won't come to any sudden conclusions and then be sorry for a whole lifetime. I am sure Walt loves you and when someone really loves you its easy to return some of that love. Russell thinks it will all soon wear off and that you and Walt are just good friends. Well enough said we will ask the Lord that His will be done in your life and in Walts."

It hurt James to hurt Maureen, but he couldn't bear to think of her married to someone who was not the right one. Maureen was a senior in college. It was natural for her to think of marriage next, but it had to be God's choice for her, not some impulse of the moment. Was he judging? But then what was a father for but to give godly advice to his children? He was not to run her life, but he couldn't be neutral or indifferent either.

In the next couple years while Russell left home for college, Maureen and Walt split up more than once before the final break came. Then she began teaching and traveling, a restless time for her and an anxious one for James. Had he and Emily brought on this aimlessness, this wanderlust, by their coolness toward Walt? She and Peggy McCartney, her best friend from college days, were never still, blowing hither and yon like a pair of lovely butterflies feeding on nectar, the sweetness of friends, pleasure, books, travel, harebrained fun.

Then before he knew it, Russell was in his last year of college. He came home for Christmas along with Maureen and Peg, making the old house vibrate with youth again.

These youngsters of theirs, how much joy they had given him and Emily. In spite of their occasional cynicism, doubts, clamorings of impatience, and his own failures along the way, they seemed to be following, however erratically at times, the call of God.

But what was this? There was to be no end of surprises. Twice now he had seen Russell talking to Peg quietly, intensely, with that gleam in his eye that James recognized all too well.

Peg, Maureen's friend, was now Russell's girlfriend.

It was to be as Maureen had often said. Her younger brother would be married first. Russell and Peggy, called Tex by James, were wed on an unbearably hot August evening in Beaumont, Texas, while James stayed at Narvon and worked. Having just come back from six weeks in Ireland, he wasn't able to ask off again from work so soon, even for a son's wedding.

Russell said with male indifference to the pomp and circumstance, "Aw, Dad, I don't care if you can't make it. Really what's a wedding? No one can visit or talk about anything that matters or even think straight. You know how it'll be, just mass confusion and heat and mosquitoes, all for a fifteen-minute ceremony."

Which were James' sentiments exactly. There was hardly a man alive, he thought, who cared much about weddings. His own, years before, had been private altogether, yet he and Emily had a good marriage, bumpy at times, but durable and strong. It wasn't a costly ceremony and reception that gave two people the glue of compassion, determination, and unselfishness which held a marriage through the years. Those qualities were learned—he knew it to be so—from parents who had practiced them. He hoped that he had been the example he should have been to his children.

Since he could not take the week off to drive to Texas and attend the ceremony, he sent Emily and Maureen with Bob and Margaret to Texas to represent the family.

Yet when the wedding evening came, he was desperately lonely and wondered if he had done right to stay behind. His only son marrying for better or worse this beautiful, green-eyed girl with the Texas drawl and the Scots-Irish name, promising to cherish and care for her forever—and he wasn't there.

But a few days later everyone returned, the newlyweds in the old Chevie of Peggy's. Russell began his first year of teaching the next morning.

A week later there was a reception for all the local folk when Peg, dressed in her gown, came downstairs looking like an Irish princess. Russell, perspiring, proud, tall, stood and introduced her to all the local friends. James knew that God was good to him. Russell needed a wife. She would stabilize him and give him something to work toward. It is not good that a man should be alone.

The family had grown and James' heart did also. There was room for Tex, another daughter. When Melissa was born two years later, he knew wherefore the title grandparents. There was nothing so grand as holding that small mortal, that tiny Hay with red fuzz and ribbon pasted on to signify her girlhood and a little crooked smile.

James and Emily in 1962.

Chapter 19

"Dad," Maureen was saying, "I've applied for an overseas job, and the only one that has answered positively is one in Beirut, Lebanon."

"Lebanon!" said James. "Is that the same Lebanon as in the Bible?"

"The very one, but it's not exactly my choice. I had my heart set on going to France and learning French." Maureen had always hankered to know another language. James would have been happy to know English well.

"Beirut is the capital city," she went on, "and it's evidently quite an international city. There's an English mission school there since 1860 where they need teachers."

James didn't think he'd ever heard of Beirut before she started talking about it in the early 1960s. For years he'd prayed for missionaries in conventional places like Africa, India, more recently Europe, Southeast Asia, but Beirut was a new one.

He discovered the whole Arab world suffered from a singular neglect of prayer, probably because it was so difficult to work in and the response was scant. Now Maureen planned to go teach for two years in this country so little you could cover it on the map with the width of a pencil and farther away than he liked to consider.

Yet he would never try to keep her home. Two years without Maureen would be lonelier than any previous separation, but

135

this time she would be going as a missionary and he could not stop her. Not if God wanted her there.

They left, Russell and Peg, Maureen, and a friend Betty Jamerson, to travel for the summer. Maureen would go on to Beirut at the end, and the others would fly back to the States. It was always a wrench to send someone to Ireland and not go along, but he did it, glad that his children were going again to the land of his birth, knowing his mother would be happy to see them. It took the edge off Maureen's farewell, that boisterous departure in New York, and he was back the next day on the assembly line, lonely for his kids, but too busy to do more than pray for them whenever they crossed his mind.

*　　　　*　　　　*

Dr. Torrey, who had been the first and only pastor of the church, had recently retired from Calvary Independent Church. James at that time was a member of the board. Now a few months later it was his turn to be the chairman of the elder board and pulpit committee, he, the least of all saints. It was something of a shock to find the responsibility for that great church in a sense resting upon him, the simple Irishman who couldn't even say anything right.

But an innate instinct for leadership surfaced. "Prayer is the biggest need we have," he told the board. "This church was born through prayer, and we can do nothing that will count unless God leads us."

They prayed together then and often, before talking about the potential pastors and planning who would hear them and report back to the committee. It seemed simple enough to listen to speakers, tally up their qualities, negative and positive, and then vote. But months went by and no one materialized who was acceptable. There were excellent speakers along the way, but each was either not interested in coming or was flawed in some way.

"We know a man can't be perfect," James reminded the board. "It's easy to be too critical. We must be open for God's man and not limit Him. But this last man had a problem I don't think we want. He seems to like the ladies too well."

No, of course, they didn't, agreed even the anxious. And so, the search continued with the church becoming more and more uncertain each week. Cliques popped up like mushrooms on a humid June day, cracks formed in the church fitly joined together, and James knew it was essential to get someone strong enough to hold it together. The ability to draw people together, the discernment and decisiveness of spiritual, responsible leadership, a certain charisma, these were not optional. They were necessary for this great church of over one thousand members. With its immense missionary program, there was no room for failure. If Calvary split, if its power was diluted, the whole world in a very real sense would feel it.

At the next board meeting James said, "We've been given the name of a man in Canada who sounds good. Who would like to go to hear him? It's over five hundred miles to his church in Willowdale."

Several men volunteered, and the next weekend they went, driving up on Saturday and staying overnight.

When he first saw Eric Crichton in the pulpit the next morning, James was surprised. Had they been led astray? The man had hair as white as new fallen snow. How old was he?

But when he stood to speak, he moved with vigor and his face was ruddy and unlined. His voice fairly boomed across the church, and though he had come as a babe from Scotland, there was a burr now and again in his words.

Strength, depth, and that indefinable quality that he had waited to find were there. James felt he had found his man, God's man he believed. Talking to him after the service, he found a rapport in matters of the Spirit—and the man was only forty-two years old in spite of his hair. When he consented to visit Calvary Church and preach, James and his friends returned with great hope.

The next weeks were filled with anticipation, then baffled disappointment as the church separated into two camps. It took all of James' diplomatic skill, of which he was not devoid, to keep sensitive persons from either leaving or dividing the church beyond the point of return. This was God's work. It could not be destroyed for the sake of any personality cults, himself included.

The board meetings were frequent and long, and James was often not in bed til midnight with the 5 a.m. alarm going what seemed like minutes later.

At one of the meetings there was a heated discussion about Mr. Crichton. "He's not a fundamendalist as Dr. Torrey was," said one. "He doesn't emphasize the blood of Christ enough."

Said another, "His messages are not the kind of teaching to which we're accustomed. I want the book studies that we had, not topical ones."

"Will he be willing to carry on the missionary program we have?" was another question.

To the best of his ability, James answered their questions. Then finally he spoke a word.

"All the questions are good and I'm glad you asked them. We need to be open and honest with one another and try to answer all the doubts we have. But let me say one thing now. It does not hinge on Mr. Crichton's messages, his age, the slant of fundamentalism that he has, his methods, but only one thing matters. Is he God's man for us? We all need to pray earnestly for God's will to be done. The effectual, fervent prayer of a righteous man availeth much. We need to open our minds to see Mr. Crichton as God sees him, not from our pet viewpoint. If we believe he is a godly man and can lead our church deeper in the knowledge of the Word, then he needs to be considered carefully. We need to pray to this end: that the mind of God will be clear to us."

The vote was to be the following Wednesday, and James had no idea how it would go. There were many, some of them old, influential members, who opposed him and only God knew what would come of this. But if Mr. Crichton were rejected, James trembled for the future of the church. Too much time had passed. It would be harder than ever to unite the people behind a single man after so many months of fragmented thought.

He prayed often that week, prayed that God would in mercy protect the work He had begun years before.

He asked David Van Ormer to lead the meeting because he felt so inadequate himself. That Wednesday night the Holy Spirit seemed to brood over the crowd gathered together. When the vote was taken and the elders had counted it, the result was handed to James.

He smiled. "I believe God in His mercy has answered our prayers," he said. "The vote is in favor of Mr. Crichton coming. I'll call him tonight and let him know the results and I believe that he'll accept the call with this majority."

Later that night he talked it over with Emily as they sat by the table and had a cup of tea. "At times like this I know that with all the confusion and division only God could do what has been done," he said. Emily knew his relief was great.

He paged through the Bible and stopped in I Chronicles 29, one of his favorite passages.

When he read, it was like poetry, his voice soft and reverent. "Thine, O Lord, is the greatness, and the power, and the glory, and the victory, and the majesty; for all that is in the heaven and in the earth is thine. Thine is the kingdom, O Lord, and thou art exalted as head above all. Both riches and honour come of thee, and thou reignest over all, and in thine hand is power and might, and in thine hand it is to make great, and to give strength unto all. Now therefore, our God, we thank thee and praise thy glorious name..."

The James Hay residence on Narvon Road.

Chapter 20

Looking back, it seemed not so long since Maureen had gone to Beirut even though she had stayed an extra year. Now this her third and final year there, she had written enthusiastically, inviting her parents to visit Lebanon during the lengthy Easter vacation with a stop in Ireland on their flight home.

Well. James didn't need to think whether they wanted to go, but managing the cost was another matter. It would take some neat budgeting. The thought crossed his mind that he could cut back on his twenty per cent tithe just for awhile—after all, the trip was in itself a kind of missionary jaunt—but as one who had been blessed beyond measure, he couldn't bring himself to do it. How could he use what was God's for something so pleasurable as a trip to the Middle East.

And by spring he was able to write Maureen, "I have most of the money for our trip. The Lord has been good. Work was better than usual this winter, this week will end the 55 hours than its 40 for the summer, really fits so well. In spite of all the meetings I felt extra well. I did tell you that before, but really I could not help but feel that God gave me the extra strength for the extra mile I had to go."

In April, 1966, the magnificent Pan Am jet squealed to a landing on the macadam at the Beirut Airport, setting James and Emily down in the East. Maureen and her friends waved wildly from the observation deck and waited as they went through customs.

Into Happiness, a ridiculously small car without brakes—
"We just shift to a lower gear," explained Maureen—they packed
themselves and set off on an adventure that James had never
thought possible, visiting a mission field and seeing the Holy
Land.

The first week they stayed at the lovely old school, the
Lebanon Evangelical School for Girls as it was officially called,
where Hazel St. John, principal and charming hostess, welcomed
them warmly. There they had a bewildering variety of new experiences.

There was dinner in a student's home, an Arab meal with
tabooli and kibbeh. To his Irish palate it seemed alien and queer,
yet wonderfully interesting.

They drove south in Happiness along the Mediterranean
coast through Zaraphath where Elijah had been fed by the widow.
They visited Tyre, where there was another mission school,
Tyre, that ancient citadel of power and wickedness. Now it was
no more than an enlarged fishing village, fulfilling Ezekiel's
prophecy, "a place for the laying of nets," where they wandered
over at least seven levels of civilization. James' knowledge of
history was blurred, but he remembered well when Maureen
pointed to the beach awash with bits of pottery and old pillars
and said, "There is where Paul and the disciples of Tyre with
their wives and children knelt and prayed on Paul's last
missionary journey."

The traffic of Beirut amused and occasionally gave him a
moment's panic. "But Dad," said Maureen, "you've got to drive
like they do. It's survival of the fittest."

They saw magnificent mountains, quaint villages, souks with
myriads of vegetables, fruits, flowers, people—ah, the people,
multitudes of them, a vast cauldron of seething humanity, and
James thought how Jesus had been moved with compassion over
the teeming crowds of people in marketplaces such as this. The
refugee camps filled with thousands of Palestinians, displaced
Arabs from Israel—had anyone ever gone in and told them even

once that Jesus loved them, that He had paid for their sin, that in their helpless, dreary, hate-ridden lives was One who cared infinitely for them? In the years after that trip, the PLO came to full maturity from those same camps and James wondered again if Jesus would not have made a difference in their lives and in the history of the smouldering East.

The second week Maureen took them south to old Jerusalem, then in Jordan, the plane carefully flying around Israel which was just a blank on the local map. James remembered how Jesus must needs go through Samaria. He, the Son of man, never avoided any man, or woman either, but came to all who would receive Him.

Perhaps the most moving moment in Jerusalem was at the sisters of Zion Church where a beautiful, austerely-dressed sister showed them the room in which Jesus had stood trial before Pilate. There was the design on the stone floor where soldiers had thrown dice idly to pass their time gambling for his garment. Few tourists were here, and in the quiet, James felt close to tears as he thought of the Savior. Here was where He, the Son of God, was beaten, mocked, scourged. He thought of the hymn, "But drops of grief can ne'er repay the debt of love I owe: here, Lord, I give myself to Thee. 'Tis all that I can do."

The week crested in a surge of joy at the Easter sunrise service at the Garden Tomb. How many years he had loved the Lord Jesus, and here he was in sight of that empty tomb from which Jesus had risen in triumph.

It **was** empty, and after the service at dawn, he and Emily stepped inside. No angel there, no apostles breathing hard from running, no Gardener walking about this morning, but he, James Hay, was here, himself irrefutable evidence of that resurrection so long ago which turned the world upside down and left it reeling in either disbelief or faith ever since, which had changed his life forever and given him a purpose and joy that he could never express in words. Standing there in that quiet tomb, he thought with awe of the price of redemption.

Their never-to-be-forgotten trip to the Middle East came to

an end all too quickly. Saying goodbye to all the dear friends they had met, James and Emily flew to Ireland where he saw his mother for the last time, in good health, her mind keen and fleet, still able to spin a story or admonish a grandchild or laugh merrily as she sat by the fire peeling a potato to eat. She was ninety-three years now, more than a score past her allotted three score and ten years. James told her of walking where Jesus had walked and he saw her face soften. "Mother, you'll be walking with Him before too long."

"Aye, I will," she said. "I'm ready."

And then they were up at dawn and Thomas and Katy took them to Shannon Airport. He tried to thank them for their big hearts and open home.

"We come and you always put up with us, Katy, and it never seems like a bit of bother to you," said James.

"It isn't," she said firmly. "Emily and ye will never want a place to stay in Ireland as long as we're here. I'll never forget the flannelgraph stories Emily told years ago on that first trip and how our weanes listened to them. And how ye've always talked about the Bible to us and took us to meetings. Now Willie tells the stories each week in St. Johnston to the children there. He accepted the Lord because of you."

"It was because of your prayers too, Katy. Your children have seen your faith."

"Aye, but your teaching and stories helped, James, yours and Emily's," she insisted.

Perhaps they had. He had prayed for his family for years, ever since that day when light had flooded his own soul, and perhaps Katy and Thomas and their family were the fruit of those prayers. Katy with her warm and simple faith had come to their family from her own lonely, motherless past, and she had made the homeplace an open house. There was a constant tide of visitors in and out for meals, for tea, for lodging.

"And Katy, thank you for what you've done for Mother all these years, you and Thomas," he went on changing the subject.

"I know it hasn't always been easy to have her here when you were raising your eight, yet you were always good to her."

"Well, James, the Good Book says to honor your father and mother. I had none to keep and so I kept her. I've never been sorry."

They had had disagreements, he knew, those two women, for their tongues were sharp, quick, to the point, but then it was over. Neither ever held a grudge nor allowed the sun to go down on anger, and it was to the credit of both of them that they had stayed friends while living together nearly three decades sharing tears, laughter, one man, and eight children.

The call came to board the plane, there was a final goodbye and then the flight up and away from the green jewel that sparkled in the afternoon sunshine as they looked back. It had been a perfect holiday, one he and Emily would never forget.

In spite of jet lag, which expression he didn't know, James was at work on the assembly line the next morning at 6:30 a.m. He wrote Maureen, "I went to work the following day after we landed except that I was a little sleepy in the morning. I really didn't mind it I had planned that as part of my routine, it worked out real well. That day we had a long meeting in the morning with Bob Ressler and that helped get the day in and it gave me a day's pay to begin to plan another trip. Where will you be so we can come to see you."

Where will you be, he said, and had no idea what the answer would be. Maureen was twenty-nine now and he wondered if she would ever marry. He remembered Walt and how the family's uneasiness had doubtless been a factor in that breakup. Had they been too critical, too cautious? There were others since then, but somehow the magic hadn't been there, and Maureen had either been bored or jilted—he wasn't honestly sure always—and now here she was a returning missionary in a few months. What next? He sensed her restlessness, her loneliness, in the midst of all those exotic scenes and experiences, and he prayed again that she might settle happily in a more conventional life.

In July she came home from Beirut full of excitement about

the Billy Graham Crusade she had attended in Wembley Stadium in London with her friend Rosalind. In fact, she said, she was sending a story to *Decision* about that occasion. When it was accepted, she was ecstatic.

Published the following November when the outer world matched the inner man in dreariness, the story brightened up an otherwise drab winter.

And that was not the end. Letters came, strange requests, job offers, a crate of oranges all came in response to the article. But the strangest was yet to come. In March the final letter arrived from one Ed Read who said he was a bachelor-farmer living with his mother in southwest Missouri. Innocuous-sounding letter, but he had enclosed a small photo inside.

"Will you answer?" asked James.

"Of course," she said airily. "I did all the others. I'ts rude not to. He sounds harmless and he's far away."

Then into the letter-writing and spring cheer that was bursting out everywhere, there came sad news from Ireland. Thomas phoned and said that Mother was gone, just two weeks short of her ninety-fourth birthday. James had never planned to go back for funerals, but this time he had to. He must go, Bob and he.

There at Galdonagh he sat in the parlor by his mother's casket and drew together all those years of living that she did, sifted through them, pulled out nuggets of joy and growth and pain and hardship, handled them, then laid them back in the casket with her as they did her glasses. They were gone, over forever, no more. He couldn't cling to the past, but how he would miss her. She had been there so long.

There was a heaviness about James when he returned to America. Such a big chunk of life was over, the end of an era, a generation.

Yet back at Narvon a new generation was moving on. He found that Ed Read had not faded agreeably, but was writing regularly to Maureen, later telephoning on Sunday nights. In August he turned up at Narvon, a man, fresh-faced and clear-voiced with integrity etched in the lines of his face and strength in the grip of his hand.

There was to be a December wedding, at home, insisted Maureen. "My happiest memories are at Narvon," she wrote from Missouri where she was working at their new house, "and I'd rather be married there than anywhere else."

"It doesn't seem, uh, right," said James.

Emily agreed. "We wouldn't have many guests here," she said. "And the house would need a lot of preparation. The church is the best place."

"I think so too," said James. "But still, well, if she wants it here, maybe we should let her, Emily."

"I guess it's a compliment to her home and—to us that she wants it here."

"Remember how we were married, Emily? Do you remember that quiet, little cremony and not even your own family there? I imagine they were a little upset too. A fancy wedding doesn't guarantee a good marriage," reasoned James.

So the invitations were sent and then there was a great clean-up at Narvon. Emily, who loved to save things, tried to sort through the accumulation of years and piled it in boxes to look at later, washed curtains, wished that the partition had been knocked down between the two living rooms, worried about the food and who was not invited and whether they'd be upset, but after all, fifty people were all the house could hold, and maybe they should have insisted on it being at the church, folk might not understand, and what would happen if it snowed and no one could come at all. It was a tense time indeed.

It snowed the day before, coating the world with white icing like a giant wedding cake and preventing any kind of rehearsal. Fifty relatives and almost-relatives packed in for the warm, simple ceremony.

It was his first-born, his daughter marrying, and no matter how happy he was for her, James could not stop the lump that kept rising in his throat as Maureen walked down the steps and across the living room. Giving her to the care of another man was harder than he thought even though he had often prayed for this day.

Later he wrote her, "So nice you are away from home so we can get letters from you again we just can't have you and the letters. Now it looks like we will have mostly letters and not you. So many times you went away, it seemed like so long a time til you would get back, this time it didn't seem like you were going away, yet it could be a long time before you are really home."

Russell, by now the father of two daughters, Melissa and Sylvia, was in the throes of winding down his years-long summer and evening career at Temple University graduate school. James could hardly believe it, that Russell, who had loathed school most of his life, had chosen to go not only to college, but now was on the verge of a master's degree in history. He was immensely proud of his son's achievement. It had been a long, difficult road for him, driving sixty miles into Philadelphia to every class, reading and writing far into the night, while attending to a teaching position at Garden Spot High School, summer jobs, new babies with advanced colic, and whenever possible, his life-long love affair with politics.

As James thought over these hard years, he knew that graduation from Temple required some special notice, not just a book or pen set, but, well, what tangible thing did Russell want probably more than anything else? The answer was easy. He talked it over with Emily and sent Russ a letter and check the next day.

"Congratulations on your great accomplishment. You deserve a lot of credit too Peg, all the lonely hours while Russ was in school and also while he sat and read an endless lot of books. Then all those papers you typed in the wee hours of the morning while the little ones slept. It was a real sacrifice on your part. Then I think of you Russ, looking back over the years a wee lonely boy going out that first day to Beartown school. The years spent there hoping it would all soon end, surely no more than eighth grade. Later heading off to college. I'm sure you had many fears that you never told us about before you went and while you were there. Then that nightmare of a summer when you worked at the silk mill at night and went to college during the day. I sometimes feel yet that we were cruel to you to let you do it. Now all these years of study at Temple. What a lot of endurance it took that long drive on winter nights, it took something above average. So to sum it up in a few words we are proud of you both. The check has strings attached, it's not to pay for the car or the house. It can only be used for a trip to Europe next summer or whenever it suits you to go..."

He knew he himself would have great enjoyment in their trip. There was no need to hoard his bit of money. "It is more blessed to give than to receive," he was wont to quote, and he knew from a lifetime of experience it was absolutely true.

Often he'd been saved from destruction, physical and spiritual, and it never ceased to humble him. The hand of God had touched him early though he hadn't always known it. Now in these mellow years James was conscious of His Shadow and he sat down under it with great delight. Yet at times the shadows turned chilly and even desolate and he longed to see, not through a glass darkly, but face to face...

Bless the Lord,

O my soul...

who redeemeth thy life

from destruction.

Chapter 21

It happened so quickly he could hardly reconstruct the events later.

James had been assigned to a new job driving a towmotor and stacking skids of dies in the vast lots outside the plant at Sperry New Holland. Getting off the towmotor, he climbed up the racks and tried to push something into place. He was holding on with one gloved hand which must have slipped, dropping him about six feet to the ground where he put out his hands to break the fall. Later he was not really sure.

Stunned, he lay there a minute or two gazing up at the bright blue May sky scooped like a bowl pouring warm sunshine over him. He must try to get up. It was no small task, for his hands were useless, one stuck out at an odd angle. He rightly guessed, judging from their appearance and the pain that both his wrists were broken. His back ached and he wondered if it too was broken. Perhaps he shouldn't walk and injure it further, but he couldn't lie there until someone missed him. That might not be for hours.

So he went, slowly, his head spinning, back to the plant about five minutes away holding his hands as still as he could, trying not to attract attention til he got to his own boss. He could never bear a lot of attention when he was hurting.

To the Lancaster General Hospital they took him, the nurse giving him something to ease the sharp pain. Soon he found himself in bed with both wrists in casts and his back with a broken vertebrae encased in a brace. There he lay, immobile, painfully helpless.

Across the room lay a young man, probably in his early thirties, grinning amiably at him. Al, an Italian Roman Catholic by religion and a reprobate by practice, was friendly and talkative, and for the next several days, James had a captive audience. Every day their conversation ended on one subject, like a compass that flew around to the North.

"Jim, I've been, I've been—well, you don't even want to hear what I've been. I tell you, man, I'm bad. I got a real problem with drinkin' and cussin'. Hi there, Sugarbun," he said to the nurse as she came with his medicine. "And women, I've had three wives now and the dame I live with isn't my wife."

James thought of the woman of Samaria. "You don't have to tell me how bad you are, Al, you haven't sinned against me. You've sinned against God. 'Against thee, thee only, have I sinned,' said David many years ago. You need to tell Him, Al, not me."

"Well, I know, I get tired of confessing to a priest. Actually I haven't been to church since hell froze over."

"You don't need a priest," James insisted. "You need Jesus, Al. If you're willing to come to Him as you are and ask Him to make you over, brand new, He will. He did it for me years ago. I'd never go back to my old life."

Al always listened respectfully and even agreed with him, but James knew that only the Holy Spirit could reach deep into the heart of this happy-go-lucky sinner. He was someone to pray for during the months of recovery ahead.

For it was indeed a long time before James felt himself again. During the next six weeks he was as helpless as Maureen's new little girl Elizabeth whose picture he wept to see when she sent it to him in the hospital. Never had he felt so humiliated and useless. He couldn't even eat alone, much less bathe or shave or dress. Emily would have to do it all and with her physical weakness and natural slowness, it would take all day just to maintain themselves.

Thomas and Katy arrived from Ireland for a six-week holiday, knowing nothing of James' injury.

"Why didn't ye phone us," asked Thomas, "and we would have cancelled our flight."

"James didn't want me to," said Emily. "He said he'd have more time than ever to spend with you, not being at work every day."

"But yourself, ye'll have a quare and busy time of it with him to take care of and us here too."

"Oh, we'll manage somehow. It's so good to see you both, and we'll just not worry about anything. You can feel at home and help yourselves," said Emily who had never in her life sounded overwhelmed or imposed upon with too many guests, nor dropped any hint at all that someone staying there was a trouble. Her big smile and easy pace made people relax, no matter how irregular the schedule and housekeeping were.

When James came from the hospital, he breathed a sigh of relief. He needed a cup of tea, a decent cup, one that was steeped in a pot and piping hot, not a tepid lukewarm cup with an insulting teabag floating aimlessly in it.

"Katy, I need a wee sup o' tae," he said while Thomas and Emily were settling him on the couch.

"Aye, James," and she scurried to make it. His spirits rose as he drank and visited with these dear ones. In fact he improved so much in the next few days that he said to Emily, "I believe we can take Thomas and Katy out to see Maureen and Ed after all."

Emily stood stock still. "Go to Missouri! Now?"

They had done lots of unexpected things in their lives and very little had ever prevented James from doing what he set out to do. But this was a little extreme. A man who couldn't so much as lift a cup of tea to his mouth was talking about a twelve-hundred-mile trip by car.

"Well, you and Thomas can drive and Katy and I will look

at the scenery," he said mischievously. "Don't you want to go to Missouri, Katy?"

"Aye, I do surely," she said without the faintest idea where it was nor how tiring the journey was.

"Can you sit that long?" wondered Emily.

"I know I can to see that new baby," he said. For his children or grandchildren James would endure any discomfort or deprivation.

But he forgot how much a trip, any jaunt, depended on him. There was food to be prepared. Emily always made fried chicken and packed fruit, cheese, and such to eat along the way. There was the refrigerator to clean out and clothes to launder and pack, much of which James did. This time he could only sit and watch while Emily tried to cope with all the details of a long journey and continue to take care of him. It all got done somehow, the doors were locked, and they were off on what was, to the Irish folk, the longest car journey they had ever had in two days' time.

It was a great moment when James, sitting in the rocking chair at Maureen's, his face unshaven and gaunt, held Elizabeth on his lap while his small namesake James stood there and watched Grampie and wondered why he had those big white casts on his arms. Yet he was as self-forgetful as ever, and in forgetting himself, he made others forget.

The injuries were a long time mending, but by the end of the summer, he was out of his brace. The doctor pronounced him able to work again and he returned to his old job on the assembly line.

For two more years he worked as hard as ever, the ten-hour days at the shop. Then his back began to ache at work once in a while. A little arthritis, he thought. It'll wear off.

It didn't though, but gradually increased in fury. It came to the point where he could not even go to church, it hurt so much to sit. What had happened?

"Maybe you did something to it helping us move last fall. You did so much heavy lifting then and had that long trip back with Ed guiding the truck," said Maureen whose family now lived across the road from him and Emily at Narvon.

"No, Tutsie, I didn't feel a thing then. This has just come on recently."

He didn't want to go to a doctor, but he had to eventually, yet all exercises and remedies proved useless. In May 1972, he went into the hospital for tests. A few days later back surgery was performed.

"Were you worried about it?" asked Russell who knew the risk in such an operation.

"The night before, I was in such pain I could hardly wait for morning to come and the operation. I'm sure I'll get better now," he said, always an optimist.

But there were months of pain ahead, diminishing so slowly that he wondered often if there was any change at all. Yet whenever anyone asked him how he was, he said invariably, "I believe I'm a little better." James was not one to recount horror stories of illness and hospitals to the unceasing stream of visitors at Narvon.

When he looked at himself in the mirror, he knew he was but a caricature of his old self, looking ten years older, much thinner, bent over perhaps never to straighten again. One day he began to help Maureen paper a bedroom. He was all too ready to stop when she, suspecting his weariness, suggested a cup of tea. He was sixty-three. Was this the beginning of his decline? Would he ever throw his grandchildren in the air or cut the grass or dig garden again?

His family wondered the same though no one spoke of it openly. To Russell and Maureen it was incredible that Dad was like this, not Dad of all people.

By the end of August he was as bent as ever, and though the pain was less acute, it was still there. Coming from the doctor one evening with the crickets fairly outdoing themselves in tuneless song, James and Emily stopped at Maureen's. The merry faces of her three small children did good like a medicine, as Solomon said, and they needed some cheer.

"What'd he say?" asked Maureen.

"He doesn't know why I can't straighten up, except that it's possible the operation just didn't succeed. He said they work in the dark, where they can't really see behind the backbone and sometimes, well, it just doesn't work," said James. He said it matter-of-factly, without a trace of self-pity in his tone, but Emily and Maureen knew how he must feel.

"Maybe you shouldn't have had surgery."

"Well, I had to. I couldn't sit or do anything then. At least I can get around now."

"Will you be able to be visitation minister for the church as Pastor Crichton asked you to do since you are retiring early?"

"No, Tuts, I can't if I'm not better than this. I just don't have any strength. I get worn out as soon as I walk a little or do anything."

It was a sad admission to make. But he went on, "I'm not bad off at all. And I think I'm a little better each day."

No one else felt sure of that at all. But there was much increased prayer in the weeks to follow, prayer from those who loved him.

One day in September he said to Emily, "Have you noticed I'm walking straighter?"

Emily, who was sorting carefully the not-so-dirty white clothes from those that were extra dirty so she could soak them, looked at him in surprise. "Why, I believe you're right," she said. "Stand there a minute. Yes, you are straighter, better than before."

"I've felt myself slowly straightening just a little and now I know it's noticeable. I'm feeling better too. What the doctor couldn't do, the Lord is doing," he said happily.

And it was so. After the lengthy stalemate he seemed to improve visibly each day with no medical reason whatever. How good God was to him.

Pastor Crichton stopped by a few months later, just when James was beginning to wonder what he was to **do** now that his

156

health was being restored. He often prayed about it, asking God to lead him clearly. He knew Proverbs, those matchless verses in chapter three, were still true. "Trust in the Lord with all thine heart and lean not unto thine own understanding. In all thy ways acknowledge Him and He shall bring it to pass." Having led him this far, the Lord would not forget him now.

The pastor came in, his face beaming, and gave him his usual gripping handshake. "Jim, I haven't forgotten that job we talked about nearly a year ago."

James thought he had had second thoughts about it, since it was so long unmentioned. He tried to make it easy for the pastor to back down.

"You've probably got someone else by now since it took me such a long time to get well. I know you have several missionaries home on furlough who could do it, much better than I could and they'd like the job. I don't really have any experience or training in visiting the elderly and sick."

The pastor smiled. "Only a lifetime of experience, Jim. There's no one I want more than you and Emily to do it. Or—do you have other plans now?"

James chuckled. "I can't think of anything I'd rather do. I've always wanted to serve the Lord as much as possible when I retired to sort of make up for the years when I couldn't"—and here the pastor laughed openly—"yet I didn't know how or where. I thought of going to Bible School and then helping on a mission field, but it's such an upheaval and Emily's health is not the best. This sounds like it was made for us."

"It was. We'll count on you. I think you'll really enjoy it and I know all those you visit will."

Then opened a chapter in James' life that contained his most contented, most fruitful years. Two days a week he visited the elderly, the shut-ins, the sick of the church. Emily often went along. He read the Bible to people and listened to their troubles. Some he transported to the doctor's; others he helped move into apartments. He even trimmed hedges for several.

157

Then the pastor asked him to take the Evangelism Explosion training and head up the outreach visitation program of the church. James refused to be the leader, but he took the training. Even though he had witnessed to hundreds over the years, he felt it was an asset to learn to incorporate the methods of EE. As he visited homes each Tuesday night, he knew it was the rarest and richest experience of all to lead others to the same Savior he had known all these years.

"No good thing will He withhold from them that walk uprightly," he had often quoted. It was true. He had everything—superb health, a warm family, satisfying work, and the joy of the Lord. What could a man want more?

Chapter 22

There was no one who had grander grandchildren, of this James and Emily were both agreed. Melissa, the first-born, was now a leggy ten-year-old, extra tall with red-blond hair and a careless smattering of freckles across her face. Some said she looked like Grampie, something about the chin and nose, but her mother's features were there too.

Sylvia, with the dark brown eyes of both her grandmothers and with Emily's unhurried habits, was growing up as slowly as she could, disliking change of any kind, and thinking a day spent at Grammie's was about the nicest thing she could do, especially since her cousins lived there now across from Gram's.

James, her five-year-old cousin, was a special friend, and he and Sylvia had great explorations, secret hideaways in the woods, and long talks. Now that it was winter they couldn't be outside as much, but Grammie's huge house was nearly as good.

Elizabeth, a year younger, was like a beautiful doll, all gold and pink and white. James could hardly keep his eyes off her at times. She was such a lovely, winsome child, so like Maureen years before and yet a trace of Grandmother Read too, the shade of her eyes perhaps and the set of her firm little body.

Michael, almost three, was a contented little boy who lived in the shadow of his sister. They had been born "thwends" as Michael called themselves, and where one was, the other wasn't far behind.

These were his grandchildren, Russell's two a dozen miles away, and now these last three living just across the road, a happiness that, however temporary, was to be enjoyed like eating strawberries or jumping in a pile of leaves, also momentary pleasures, yet all the more cherished for their very brevity's sake.

Christmas had come and gone, always a sparkling jewel to crown the year. January, the longest month of the year, was over, and now only a few gray days of February to be got through before spring fever would make a full attack. James and Emily with a friend had dropped in to see Maureen and the children while Ed was at work one evening. They were all clean and shining from their baths, all talking at once. Elizabeth, dressed in a fetching pink nightgown with eyes even larger than usual, carried a tiny ladybug from the drape where a colony of them seemed to have lodged for the winter, and showed it to the guest who sat in bemused fascination watching this self-possessed small girl.

She was extra tired, was Elizabeth, and she needed to be in bed soon, said Maureen, so they did not linger.

It was in the wee hours of the morning, he was never sure what time exactly, when James woke with the wind howling coldly after the unseasonable warmth. He looked outside through the swaying trees and to his utter horror, he saw two ambulances and a police car sitting in front of Maureen's house.

"Emily," he gasped, shaking her awake. "There's trouble across the road. Must be little James, he gets such attacks of asthma and croup. They were okay earlier—or maybe it's Maureen or Ed who is ill."

Those dreadful red lights kept flashing rhythmically like menacing eyes peering into the night. His clothes he threw on in seconds and was out the door. O God, I hope little James is okay, but don't let Maureen get sick either—could it be Michael, he's such a little boy yet—maybe Ed had a heart attack, many men do—it can't be Elizabeth at least, she's too healthy.

But it was. Surrounded by the ambulance crew, Elizabeth was spreadeagled on the floor, the little pink nightgown cast off in a heap beside her, and the beautiful face the color of skimmed milk. The family—where was Maureen? Huddled in the other bedroom, they sat too shattered to think, with disjointed prayers and cries and a horrifying numbness.

It was over so quickly and with such finality. At the hospital Elizabeth was pronounced dead with an overwhelming virus of which no one was sure what it was. Would it affect the little boys or Ed who had kept her alive til the ambulance came?

Whatever it was, the death-angel had come only for Elizabeth and with astonishing swiftness. A form of encephalitis was one verdict, but Maureen and Ed privately believed it was Reyes Syndrome that had taken her.

"In everything give thanks, for this is the will of God in Christ Jesus concerning you," said James wrapping his arms around Maureen as she and Ed returned that morning from the hospital. He knew better than to question God. A lifetime of trust could not be overcome by what seemed an act of senseless caprice. There was a purpose that perhaps only Heaven knew. He would trust.

Yet in this mortal world is there any sorrow quite like the sorrow of a child's death? James and Emily both knew there were horrors worse, but in those days when only two small boys walked in their front door without a dancing little girl alongside, they wondered what they could be.

It turned out to be the first desolation in a decade of decline and death, for in the next years the circle around the table at Christmas dinner kept decreasing. Who would have thought that Elizabeth, nearly the youngest and apparently the healthiest of the clan, would be the first to leave? Following her was Sadie, Emily's younger sister, Sadie with the loving heart; then Curtis, a big brother; and Mary, the oldest sister, a whole generation of Russells slipping away.

James did not fear getting old—he would not want to repeat any of the years he'd lived—yet it was with astonishment that

161

he turned seventy and knew that he'd lived his allotted three score and ten. Where had the years gone? From now on it was borrowed time for him, yet his strength, like Caleb's, was not diminished.

But Emily, he watched her decline gradually like the old eight-day clock on the bookcase, just running down. Her heart began to weaken, further complicated by diabetes which had prevented her from going on the last trip to Ireland.

That had been a hardship, to leave her behind at the last minute, she who so loved going to the Old Country, while he went away to fulfill a promise to help some missionaries in Drogheda near Dublin. It had been in many ways a bleak six weeks there in that cold damp building working long hours while back at Narvon the worst winter in years set in.

"Peg and the girls were here Sunday and helped me sweep the snow off the flat roof. She told me I shouldn't be up there in case I got dizzy, but I felt okay. Then it snowed again a couple days later and had to be done again," Emily wrote.

He knew she shouldn't be sweeping and shoveling snow, not with those swollen legs of hers, but she'd done it always, and found it exhilarating. Emily had never worked conventionally, yet she could rise to an occasion beautifully, be it a snowstorm, a leak in the pipes, or a grandchild who needed someone to look at the encyclopedia with him.

When he got home from Ireland, he made up his mind he'd not go back again without her. Katy and all the dear ones there told him to bring Emily next time.

She seemed better, the diabetes controlled largely by diet, when he returned. But his brother Bob was nearly bedfast now with the ugly emphysema that was destroying his lungs, the result of many years' work handling asbestos.

Bob, his protective elder brother, was reduced to a panting skeleton, yet his dark brown eyes glowed with light when anyone he loved walked into the living room. There wee Maggie had set up a hopsital of sorts giving constant care with even an oxygen tank for those times when he feared he would lose his breath altogether.

That last great enemy was stalking him and it broke James' heart to watch. Yet as Bob's body had weakened these last years, his tongue, always reticent, had loosened, and for the first time Bob expressed his faith openly. He read everything he could lay his hands on until he got too weak, and James knew that Bob truly knew and loved Christ.

It was an immense comfort to him as he watched the end come.

Yet there were to be other burdens at the same time. One early day in November when a golden haze lay in the valley and James felt relaxed and even a little lazy, Emily said, "James, I feel dizzy. I don't believe I can walk very well."

She couldn't indeed, and he persuaded her to go to the doctor who said she must go straight to the hospital. It looked like she was verging on a stroke, or perhaps even having one. James knew it ran in the family and he prodded her to waste no time.

"But James, I've got to have some decent nighties. I can't go with these," she said.

"Why can't you?"

"Well, I just can't. Couldn't we stop on the way and get a couple? It won't take long."

James knew better, but he also knew Emily would have it no other way. She could be as calmly obstinate as an Irish donkey on occasion. This was one of the occasions.

When they finally got to the hospital, the specialist was irate, having expected the lady to arrive long before. "You could have died," he said icily.

Then he put her into intensive care for several days until it was decided she must have a pacemaker. How amazing the medical perceptions are, thought James, who respected a surgeon's skill, remembering that simple surgery on his appendix years before which had saved his life.

It was a bleak November. Emily spent her birthday in the hospital and was still there on Thanksgiving. It was the first one since anyone could remember that she hadn't fed the clan. She was improving though, that toughness of hers rising once again to push her back into her quiet routine.

But on the thirtieth day of the month, Bob left, not in a paroxysm of choking as everyone feared, but so quietly even wee Maggie did not see him leave. She stepped into the kitchen, and when she came back seconds later to see if he wanted a poached egg, he wasn't there.

*   *   *

There seemed to be a lull in the inexorable march of illness and death in the clan. The next year James began to think of another trip to Ireland, this time with Emily along. It might be their last one together.

Then suddenly surgery loomed again with frightening implications, a lump on her breast requiring a mastectomy. A family council was called.

"Won't it be awfully hard on you, Mom?" wondered Maureen.

James hated the thought of the mutilation and the pain. Would the surgery really help? The word cancer was worrisome.

But Russell said, "Aw, Mom's tough. She'll make it. Of course you should have surgery, Mom. I mean, fight it with all you've got. They do great things at the hospital today."

And Russell, who probably understood her better than anyone else, was the prevailing influence. Emily had the surgery and to everyone's astonishment, she recovered and was herself sooner than even she thought, except for the unsightly swelling in her left arm.

"Next year," said James, "Next year we'll go to Ireland for sure, God willing." Spring, he thought, when the whin bushes are blooming and they're cutting turf and there's hardly any night, that's when we'll go. We'll see primroses and I'll fish in the lake.

And, like Paul, he wanted to see how the believers were doing, in particular the little church that met on the old Rooskey farm where he had grown up.

In early February he bought tickets though Emily kept saying she thought perhaps she shouldn't go. She just didn't feel all that well.

"Well, I'm not going without you," he said. "We'll just plan on it until God stops us."

It was a Tuesday evening in late February, the day after Elizabeth's death-day though no one realized it til later, that Emily and her sister Ruth went to Dee's house for supper. James was away all day until ten that evening doing his regular visitation for the church. When he got home, he found Emily on the couch shivering with her coat on.

"I can't seem to get warm," she said. "At Dee's I started shaking, but I didn't want to tell her—she had such a good meal. And I was so tired I could hardly move."

"No tea, Tuts?" he said after he had covered her with some blankets.

"No, I'm too tired. Just let me lie here til I get warmer and a little more rested."

He was concerned though he knew it was not unusual for Emily to lie down and say she wanted to rest awhile. Often he went to bed with her lying there reading the paper and snoozing in turn. Sometimes she would get up later and start baking or write a letter. Her schedule had always been unorthodox and he had long since given up trying to make her conform to his routine.

But to his shock, early the next morning when he woke, she was still on the couch, burning with fever, and scarcely seemed to be coherent. When he tried to persuade her to sip water or juice, she would turn away and moan.

"Could I take you to the doctor, Emily?" he said.

"No, just let me lie a little. So tired," she would mutter. He managed to get her big coat off and covered her with several wool blankets. All day he stayed near her, phoning the pastor that he couldn't make it to Lancaster that day.

When Maureen came from school, she took her temperature and found it was nearly 104 degrees. Between them, they managed to get her to the doctor who said, after probing and testing, that it was probably a bad case of flu and she could go home, take liquids and aspirin, or go to the hospital for tests. It was definitely not her heart acting up.

"I want to go home," Emily managed to say and even seemed a little brighter.

The next morning though, the fever was higher again, and she could keep nothing in her stomach. James had never seen anyone so sick before, her temples pounding, her mouth dry and fuzzy, a little moan with every breath.

"She'll dehydrate, Dad," said Maureen. "We've got to get her to the hospital."

The ambulance came, and for the next two days and nights Emily lay in the hospital scarcely conscious, moaning, getting weaker every moment, with tubes and needles everywhere. No one knew what to do for her.

She was dying, he knew, and it was an ugly, dreadful death grasping at her, gripping, holding tight, squeezing all the pain and torment it could from her. How could it have come so quickly?

She seemed to be going fast on Saturday morning when her kidneys slowed down. She was bloated and twisted by misery almost beyond recognition.

He phoned Maureen. "She's going, Tutsie, her kidneys aren't working."

"Oh, Daddy, that's how Granny Russell went."

"I know," he said, his voice breaking.

"I'll be right in," she said.

About noon Russell came striding into the hospital room,

back from a trip, and stopped in horror. As he took Emily's hand, she opened her eyes and smiled at her son, the first smile anyone had seen that day, then drifted off again moaning and tossing.

It was probably only a matter of hours now, but did there have to be so much pain? She cried out when the nurse touched her, that bloated body sensitive to even the pressure of the bed. Couldn't someone give her a shot to ease her?

Then a specialist turned up and though he was short on manners, he had a hunch. "It looks like it could be a severe blood infection," he said. "We could try penicillin."

It would seem, thought James, that it was too late to try, that it would simply prolong the agony. Yet they must try to do something, even a brief relief.

And with the first drop in her veins, Emily began to come back from the brink. Almost afraid to believe it, James watched the miracle with his children. For a miracle it was to all those who had seen her.

James and Emily could go on living at the old brown house at Narvon.

Now he was past seventy, yet his strength, like Caleb's, was not diminished. Every day was precious. There was so much to do—reading, painting the house, visiting, talking to his grandchildren, and always witnessing to those who didn't know his Joy, his Life-center, Jesus Christ, the one who gave meaning to his life and hope to his future...

Bless the Lord, O my soul...
who satisfieth thy mouth
with good things so that
thy youth is renewed
like the eagle's.

Chapter 23

Waking at six, James lay in bed a moment, listening to a score of birds sing and a horse and buggy clop by the house. It was early to hear that; most Amishmen were still milking. Then he sat on the edge of the bed, scratched absentmindedly a moment, and got up. On these midsummer days he could hardly wait to see the morning.

He walked quietly downstairs and outside, a tryst he kept with the morning every day of the year, but especially enjoyable on such as this. Behind the house a mist rose through the woods with the sun like arrows of light piercing through it. A couple rabbits sat among the remains of the bean row, watching him with their black eyes shining and noses twitching. They knew he was harmless. James might have tried to shoot them had it not been for his grandchildren—they liked them—and so the bunnies were secure.

Back inside the house, he ate a bowl of cereal, then spread out his Bible on the table beside the kitchen window. After forty years of punching a time-clock, he cherished the leisure of early morning. His mind was fresh and he could read and pray clearly.

But even in prayer, he could not express himself as he wanted, yet he opened his heart wide and let God see all the praise and adoration and simple thanksgiving that were there. How could he ever tell Him all that He meant?

Psalm 103 came to mind.

Bless the Lord, O my soul, and all that is within me, bless His holy name. Bless the Lord, O my soul, and forget not all His benefits... What multiplied benefits he had, did ever a man have more, home and Emily in it, health, a satisfying job, complete joy within, grandchildren, that ruby-throated hummingbird there at the window sucking nectar from the petunias in the box, a right spunky fellow who must need prodigious amounts of energy to spin his wings like that, his church, his friends, his God.

Who forgiveth all thine iniquities...it was Jesus' blood that made it possible to be forgiven, the Sacrifice to end all those sacrifices of the Old Testament, and now not one sin was put to his account. If the Son shall make you free, you shall be free indeed; there was no guilt for him.

Who healeth all thy diseases...his own back, healed completely now, and Emily's illness also, so that she was still here with him, he could hear her stirring upstairs.

Who redeemeth thy life from destruction...how many times his life had been saved, that time years before when he fell at work among all those high voltage wires and not one ever touched him, the brush with death in the hospital, and all the times he must have been saved from destruction and never even knew it, when he traveled, worked, drove the car.

Who crowneth thee with loving-kindness and tender mercies...always tender was God, and His mercies were new every morning, great is Thy faithfulness.

Who satisfieth thy mouth with good things so that thy youth is renewed like the eagle's...good things, and he thought of tea and potatoes and Irish scone with raisins, and playing kickball with his grandkids, and picking blackberries...he must do that today...it all helped to renew his youth, nothing like children around to make a man feel good, thank You, Lord that they're here with us.

The mercy of the Lord is from everlasting to everlasting upon them that fear Him and His righteousness unto children's children... Unto children's children. That was Missy, Sylvia, James, Susan, Michael. He named each one and prayed that they might always seek God's righteousness above all else, and then he prayed for the new little girl Anne who was to come from Korea and join Maureen and Ed's family.

James went through his prayer list, missionaries, pastors, friends, the dear ones in Ireland...until he heard a little tap on the window. There was Michael with his big smile, an exceedingly dirty shirt, and a bucket with two eggs rolling precariously around. It was evidently his day to feed the chickens.

"How are ye, Mickey?" he said as he pushed up the window.

"Okay." Michael was a man of few words.

"Are you coming in for breakfast?"

"No, it's not my turn. It's Susan's."

"How about a quick glass of orange juice before she comes?"

"Okay," gladly spoken. And he ran around to the back door and into the kitchen.

"How are your chickens?"

"Pretty good. I wish we had babies though. They're cute." A pause. "Is Grammy asleep?" Mike and Grammy had a special kinship.

"No, she's awake, I think, but not dressed yet."

"Well, I gotta go." Grampy gave him a hug and watched him go out the door. It was the first of a dozen visits that day. Mike was in and out.

It was only minutes til Susan appeared, Susan who came from Viet Nam to become the boys' sister just a year after Elizabeth's death. She was twelve now and prettier every day, a sparkling girl who had given a new dimension to Maureen's family. Watching her grow up, James knew again that God's ways are perfect.

Susan helped him set the table and fry the bacon. "Say, I've got some mushrooms. Would you like me to fry those?" asked James in a conspiratorial tone of voice. "We won't tell anyone."

171

Susan's almost-black eyes shone. She loved these breakfasts with Grampy, every third Saturday was her turn, for you never knew what you might have.

"Umm, sounds good," she said as James rummaged in the refrigerator for them.

They dropped the mushrooms into the pan along with the eggs, added a dash of salt and pepper, set the tea to steep, and made toast.

Susan, who, like the hummingbird feasting at the window-box, was a flame of energy, relished every mouthful. It was delightful to have Gramp's undivided attention in this old cool kitchen with her favorite creatures, birds, just outside.

Then he got his Bible. "What shall we read today, Susan?"

"I like the story of Peter in prison."

"Okay, we'll read that one."

They each read half of it, and Susan, listening, liked the soft, reverent tone of Grampy's voice. She knew he loved God more than anything else—you could just tell by the way he talked and she had never really seen him angry. She guessed he never was.

They prayed each in turn, and Grampy, listening, marveled at the simple faith of this child. Her prayers were natural, perceptive, never trite.

"Well, Susan, I guess I have to get ready to go away. What are you doing today?"

"We've all got chores to do. It's cleaning day."

"Oh, so it is. Maybe you could dust for me later today." He walked with her to the door (Grampy always treated everyone like a special guest) and she waved her smooth brown arm back at him. "I'll get your mail for you," she called back.

Emily, who had stayed discreetly upstairs til the private breakfast was over, appeared. She was nearly her old self again. After a second cup of tea with her, James left for Lancaster.

There with two other men, he helped old Mrs. Peterson move to an apartment, a job complicated by some unusually narrow

172

steps and the lady's piano with which she could not part. James' broken back had come a long way.

On his way home he stopped at the Fairmount Nursing Home where two of his people lived whom he visited regularly, along with Lock Whitaker who had been his longtime neighbor on the Narvon Hill. A catnap in the car before he went in kept him from getting heavy-eyed while he chatted with them.

Driving along Route 322, past a clutch of cantelope vendors, mostly Mennonite children sitting in the back of wagons with melons piled around them, he came across a hitchhiker, a young man with a beard. James hardly ever turned one down. It was a chance to witness.

"Where you going?" he asked the boy.

"To Honeybrook."

"Well, I'll take you as far as Beartown and maybe you'll get another ride. Hop in." Then he asked some questions about his interests and job.

Finally he brought up the subject that was always in his mind. "You said you went to church. But I wonder if you were to die, what answer would you give if God said to you, 'Why should I let you into my Heaven?'"

It was a startling question, but so kindly asked that the boy, after pausing in amazement a moment, said, "Well, I'd tell Him I had joined the church and done my best all my life."

"That's fine, son. But God doesn't really care how much you try to be good or go to church. The only thing that matters with Him is what you've done with His Son. The Bible says we've all sinned and we need cleansing. Only Jesus' blood can do that. You have to accept Him and He makes you fit to live in Heaven—and fit to live on earth too." Then he told what had happened to himself many years before, how he had come to Christ, a story as fresh as the day it happened to him, and the youth listened carefully.

It was time to drop him off and turn up the Narvon Road. He stopped by the edge of the road and said, "Son, I'll pray for you that you'll truly know Christ as your Savior. He can answer a lot of those questions you have. And read the New Testament, a couple chapters a day. You'll find Him there."

He shook hands, gave him a tract, and drove home, praying silently. The Word of God never returns void, he thought.

As he drove in the driveway and under the old maple tree, he found twelve-year-old James sitting on the porch with a book. "Say, James, my boy, let's pick blackberries. I've never seen such big ones as are at the Old Place."

They **were** enormous, great clumps of them, and he could easily fill a quart box standing in one place. Even young James, not usually given to such a pastime, enjoyed it, but then most things were fun with Grampy. The sun was hot, but for a change there was no humidity, and overhead clouds billowed across the sky as though an angel, cleaning house, were sweeping the dust across the universe.

"Grampy, I have three boxes full."

"That's great, James, I have some too. I guess we'll soon stop. Do you suppose your mother will make some pies for us?"

"Umm, she will and Grammy will make jam. She likes to do it. Did you have blackberries in Ireland, Gramp?"

"Aye, we did. That's how I first earned money. I got two shillings for a stone of berries. That's like a bucket's worth."

They walked companionably back to the car listening to the crickets and watching out for snakes. The old barn stood there, its unpainted wood darkened from the sun and weather, a silent witness of all the living that had once been done there and now was no more. James remembered fifty years before when he had first come here with Emily and all the activity in this lovely little glen. How dreary, how utterly morbid it would be to get old if he didn't know God who is ageless. In knowing Him there was no fear, no looking back. He glanced at the sky and thought as he did nearly every day, O Lord Jesus, how long, how long, ere we hear the glad song: Christ returneth? The older he got, the more he longed to see Him, to **know** Him face to face.

174

He thought of those, some more dear than his own life, who knew not his joy. If only he could make it clear what he knew but could never adequately explain to others. How empty and pointless life was without Christ. How rich and worthwhile and **wonderful** it was with Him.

*　　　*　　　*

That evening after their light supper, James said to Emily, "Let's take a walk."

In the dusk a moon was hanging low as they followed the road through the woods to the clay mine, and lightning bugs winked at them. They walked slowly, Emily unable to go fast, and unwilling had she been able. She liked to look at flowers and bugs and trees.

"There's a robin singing his goodnight song," she said stopping to listen.

He waited with her. Then they began to climb the steep rough road to the top of the hill from where they could see the Conestoga Valley stretched out before them. Tiny fields of a dozen shades of green and gold filled the valley, dotted with barns and silos, all with impeccable German tidiness.

James took her arm to help her over the stones, that arm that was always swollen now from her surgery, and they stood there on top of the hill looking at the valley fade into darkness and the lights appear—like the light of the gospel, thought James, glowing steadily here and there, the only true Light that lighteth every man that cometh into the world.

And looking over the valley, he thought too that it was rather like their lives, his and Emily's, the valley of the years so soon over and now they were climbing, climbing the last lap. Their perspective was clearer now, truer, and looking back they could even begin to see the beauty of all the way He had led them, the heartbreaks and starkness softened and covered by the rich growth. Was that like Heaven, only more so? A sense of His

175

hand upon all of life and wondrous good coming from even the horror and sadness of life? It had to be. God would have to make it up, somehow, somewhere.

His mind went back again to Psalm 103. "He hath not dealt with us after our sins, nor rewarded us according to our iniquities. For as the heaven is high above the earth, so great is His mercy toward them that fear Him. Bless the Lord, O my soul."

It was nearly dark by now and they hadn't seen a deer, but a couple rabbits ran down the road in front of them. He and Emily walked hand in hand over the rough spots. She was still at his side. Each day, each hour was His gift to them.

As they neared the house, their pace quickened. "I believe McConaghays are there," said Emily. "I thought they might be over tonight."

They went inside and had tea with scone and fresh blackberry jam.

Chapter 24

How could fifty years have slipped along so easily, like a tale that is told, said the Psalmist. Yet not so easily either, plenty of bumps, illnesses, financial crunches, heartaches, but all cushioned with a multitude of blessing. Today the blessings prevailed.

Thus James thought as he and Emily celebrated their golden anniversary on a warm mellow Saturday afternoon, November 10, 1984, fifty years to the day, at Calvary Church. Peggy made a wondrous cake decorated for the occasion. And Emily wore a new dress the color of the sea.

It was indeed a golden day in their golden years as crowds of family and friends dropped in to wish them well.

The next years passed even more quickly as James continued the visitation ministry at the church two or three days a week. He was older than many of the folk he visited. He wondered how long he should continue. Pastor Crichton was soon to retire from the church. Should he, James, retire also? He loved the work and Emily did too though it was getting more difficult for her now when she accompanied him. Her memory was starting to fail and it was hard for her to enter into conversations when she felt disconnected and left out.

One warm June evening in 1987 as he pulled into his driveway, he was met by Maureen.

"Mom is lying at the back of the house where she fell probably an hour ago, maybe longer. I think she's broken her hip," she said.

"The ambulance should be here any minute."

He quickly pulled the car out of the way and parked. "Well, Tuts, what happened?" he asked, hunkering down beside Emily.

"I was hanging up clothes and must have caught my heel. All at once I was down. Maybe I can get up if you'll help me." But she couldn't. It wasn't safe even to try.

"How long were you here?" he said.

"Oh, I don't know. I just watched the clouds go by—they're so beautiful—and the planes were coming in to Philadelphia, one after another. I'm glad it wasn't cold or rainy," she said.

He was glad too. What if he had stayed in Lancaster through the evening, as he often did, to do outreach visiting? Emily had been all right when he phoned her about 5 p.m., just two hours before. What if Maureen hadn't come over?

The ambulance took her to the hospital where x-rays showed she had cracked her pelvis in two places. It would be a long convalesence.

James knew then he had his direction. He phoned the pastor about the accident and said he would need to be with Emily from now on, that God had shown him clearly in this way. Emily needed him. He would miss the work with the church—these had been his happiest years—but the will of God was all that ever really mattered.

And so for the first time since he came to America, James stayed home every day. Yet he was hardly idle. Just the day after Emily arrived home from the hospital, his niece Anne Thompson and her family, six altogether, came from Ireland for a three-week visit and stayed in their big house. What with looking after Emily and visiting with them, James' days were full indeed.

When the Irish guests left, life fell into a pattern. James rose, sometimes before dawn, and sat at the kitchen table reading and praying. He had a host of people, mostly missionaries, but others too, to pray for.

When he heard Emily stirring, he would help her. The hip was painful but mended more rapidly than anyone expected.

178

The Gerry and Anne (Hay) Thompson family from Ireland visiting James and Emily Hay in Pennsylvania. Anne is James' niece.

The day was full of small homely tasks.

One of the bright spots of each day, one that was never routine, was evening tea at 9:30 when some or all of Maureen's youngsters would come across the road and join him and Emily. He gave them tea and scone, served with blackberry jam, love, warmth, Bible verses, and good humor. It kept him young to have teenagers underfoot, telling funny stories, asking advice, laughing.

By now even the youngest child Anne Marie, who had come one Christmas from Korea, was allowed to join in the teas, Anne with the glowing cheeks and infectious laughter. What memorable times these were. The evening would conclude when Michael played the organ, old hymns like "Jesus Paid It All." He had a sensitive touch, did Michael. James and Emily, holding hands, sat on the couch and watched as he played. It was beyond James that anyone would not prefer such melodic hymns, rich in truth, to many of the modern, tiresome, repetitive songs that seemed to be popular.

James and Emily Hay in 1987.

One morning near the end of August, they went across the road, Emily slowly with her walker, to say goodbye to James, their oldest grandson, who was reluctantly leaving for Wheaton College. They were proud of him, a National Merit Scholar, but wondered for the thousandth time where the years had gone. Next year it would be Susan who planned to go to Moody Bible Institute.

Through the autumn Emily improved so much that she no longer needed the walker. But her memory worsened, that sharp clear mind of hers which the family had often laughingly likened to an elephant's memory. The winter came on bleakly, and the days grew short. She fell into depression and old fears overtook her. She cried often and would not be comforted. Had James lost his sweetheart of over fifty years? She was the only one he'd ever really had.

180

Every morning and night James continued to read the Bible and pray with Emily, hoping and believing as he did that the darkness would pass. And as spring came on, it did indeed seem to lighten. "The Lord my God will enlighten my darkness," said David in the Psalms. The Word of God was the only hope a man had in this life to help him through the shadows. He tenderly waited, and gradually as summer came on, the worst of the heaviness seemed to pass, though Emily's memory still kept slipping.

Thus it fell on James now to maintain the house, both inside and out, prepare meals, clean, do laundry, trim hedges, repair, bake scones, and even make jam.

Yet his longing to tell others of Christ had never waned. Now that he was confined at home, he could no longer visit and reach out personally. Was there another way to tell of the goodness and grace of God?

A ministry by mail, called the Mailbox Club, had begun for him several years before on a small scale. Now it began to expand during these home-bound years as more and more names came to his attention. Each day James sent Bible lessons to people who requested them. As one lesson was finished, he would correct it and return it along with a new lesson until the series was completed.

As he sent the lessons, he often added a note of encouragement, sometimes writing a whole letter especially to prisoners, of whom he had a good number. These were men whom he would never know on earth, but how wonderful to meet them one day in Heaven. Wrote one, "I'm glad that I had a chance to do these lessons from you, Jim. I learned a lot...when the time comes that I get a chance to go home with Christ in my life I know I won't be back...But I will never forget this time in my life because this is where I was reborn with the Lord and became a new and true Christian...."

Another wrote, "I was sentenced to 17 years in the state prison. I became reacquainted with the Lord on January 6, 1989, here at the city jail...Jesus Christ means the world to me right now. I agree with the Apostle Paul that a door had been opened for me in the jail and prison ministry...."

His heart ached for them all, young men mostly, who had lost so much, yet they had gained everything in Christ. The ways of God are past finding out.

By now James was eighty years old, and yet he was still allowed to serve God, the Lord, his Savior and Friend. His life was quiet, but full.

Every Sunday afternoon Russell and Peggy came to see them. It was good to have a tall strong son to help with the house. He even put on a new roof that summer, walking calmly up and down the steep slope while James, who could never bear heights, handed him the new shingles from the flat roof. It was a relief when the job was finished and Russell back on earth again.

Then Russell's oldest daughter Melissa was married and it seemed but a few days since James had first held her and laughed at the bow pasted on her hair. What a beautiful bride she was. That same spring her sister Sylvia graduated from Lebanon Valley College with a major in Spanish, a language she could probably speak better than James could English. He was proud of his grandchildren, but he also feared for them. Life today had more risks than walking on the roof. He longed for them, each one, to know and follow the Lord Jesus, to hunger and thirst for righteousness, to seek after God with their whole heart. Not wealth, not education, not even health, but knowing God was all that mattered for them in this life and in the life to come.

That life could not be far away, he often thought. Emily was more weary and frail each day. His patience ran thin sometimes with repetitive conversations, the sameness of each day, yet each morning he sat by the kitchen window and reached around the world in prayer. His joy was in God.

Chapter 25

Emily wasn't eating. The malady, whatever it was, came on her just days after Susan's marriage to Thomas Hsieh on December 28, 1991.

Getting to the wedding had taken all of James' energy and wiles. Emily said she didn't want to go and she didn't know what to wear and why couldn't she just stay home. But she couldn't be left alone and James sorely wanted to see Susan married. During the ceremony Emily's gift of smiling did not fail her, but nonetheless it was an exhausting day for her.

There was a homemade dinner later in the day at the big brown-shingled house for fifty guests, mostly Thomas' Taiwanese family in from the Midwest. James enjoyed the evening of celebration and a final lingering chat with Thomas and Susan before they left. Every bedroom was full that night with family and guests.

Three years before, Maureen and her family had moved from across the road into half of the brown house with Emily and James. It was again a double house with some connecting overlap. Though they lost a measure of privacy, it was a relief to James to have the Reads beside them especially since Emily had just had two stays at the hospital that same summer. The vigor of the grand-children was cheering, and the clatter they made was good company. Anne, a vibrant teenager by now, was in and out often,

James and Emily with their son Russell, daughter-in-law Peg, daughter Maureen, and son-in-law Ed Read in December 1991.

especially at the 9:30 tea time. The rest came and went—to Wheaton, to California, and to Chicago.

Now three years later he was even gladder to have the family living so near. Emily had never been without an appetite before. The doctor said it could be cancer. Did they want all the tests and treatment put into motion? With Emily's mind so muddled and her body so frail, James said no. He wanted Emily at home with him where they could talk and touch each other and see the grandchildren and watch the birds outside the window.

One Sunday afternoon in mid-January James sat at the kitchen table writing a letter while Emily lay on the couch in the next room. It was thus more and more. She had little strength to sit up but instead would lie watching the clouds and trees through the south window. As long as he was in sight, she was content.

As he wrote, James suddenly noticed a man walk past the kitchen window toward the road. He didn't recognize him but noted he was tall and in casual clothes. The man walked easily, not hurried, and he kept glancing in toward Emily's window where she lay. It was unusual for a man to walk out the drive, not in from the road. Where did he come from? There was nothing but woods behind the house.

James went immediately to the front door to greet him, but when he stepped to the side of the porch, no one was in sight. He looked the length of the driveway, but it was empty. He hurried to the back of the house, and no one was there.

He came slowly back inside and sat by Emily. She talked, as she loved to do, about the days when they were at Bloomfield together, when they were courting. Soon Russell and Peg came to visit as they usually did on a Sunday.

James did not mention the stranger who had just walked by, but he pondered it often in the following days. Was this one of those wee warnings, of which his mother used to speak, a hint that things would not continue as they were? Had they been visited by one who was given charge over them, by a ministering spirit? Was the man an angel?

Emily's decline was steady. She marveled at her inability to eat, but with her fading memory she lost perspective of the length of time and didn't worry overly much. James spent his days trying to make something look appetizing to her.

Saturday, February 15, 1992, he and the family set up a hospital bed downstairs by the same south window where Emily could look outside. James would sleep on the couch at night. Maureen helped with bathing and dressing before she went to school each morning. As the week progressed, the nights and days got worse. James was up and down constantly to help her.

Tuesday evening they read as usual from the Bible. Emily read from Romans 8, clearly and with great expression, "For I reckon that the sufferings of this present time are not worthy to be compared with the glory which shall be revealed in us." She read it again—and then the third time as though to impress it on her mind.

The next day she had a stroke. It was the last day she got out of bed.

That night she was wakeful and alert. James stood by her bed. He patted her and held her hand and kissed her like a bride. They laughed together and remembered the beautiful days gone by. Maureen, who was temporarily sleeping nearby, heard and came in.

"I see sparks, beautiful lights," said Emily. She waved her hand futilely when James asked her to describe them. "It's so beautiful I can't tell you."

Later she said, "I saw a great crowd of people and a Man with them. He looked at me and said, 'You're coming too.' And I was encouraged."

"That was Jesus," said James and held her hand tightly. He marveled at her smile. He had never seen her so lighthearted, so joyful in all their lives together. What must the Fountain be like when the spray at the edge is so incomparable?

As the night wore on, the glory dimmed and pain increased. Emily had entered the Valley of the Shadow. Thursday was a difficult day. Maureen stayed home from school. Russell and Peg with their girls were there that evening.

There had to be help to get through the night. When they phoned him, the doctor reaffirmed that little could be done except to make her comfortable. He prescribed medication for pain, and she finally fell asleep. James himself slept that night but woke several times to look at her. Her breathing was strong, but she was so quiet. He missed her already.

On Saturday Emily was aware of each one for the last time, Maureen as she washed her face, James when he helped turn her, and Russell when he arrived early in the day. Her eyes caught and connected with each one. She began to withdraw. They talked to her less and less. No one would keep her now. There was a sense of angels very near.

On Sunday early in the morning, Maureen rushed downstairs. The breathing pattern seemed different, and she phoned Russell.

But Emily leveled out and continued as before. James sat by her side that day except for a nap. He told Russell and Maureen about the man in the driveway for the first time.

"That was a month ago today," he said. They talked quietly and seemed nearly to hear the sound of wings. There was an amazing sense of expectancy.

Just after the clock struck five that Sunday afternoon, Emily left. The three of them, James, Russell, and Maureen, were alone together by her bed. They watched Emily, ever so quietly, move on to that great unseen world where there is no night, no sorrow, where all tears are wiped away, where Jesus and so many dear ones already were. It was February 23, the same day four-year-old Elizabeth had left eighteen years earlier. Was she waiting for Grammy? Heaven seemed almost palpable.

In the next weeks it was not so much grief as a sense of emptiness and loneliness that filled James. He couldn't wish her back, but how he missed her. As he remarked to Maureen, "So many times she's not there." What did she look like? What must her smile be now? All the aches and weariness and misunderstandings washed away, and only clarity and wondrous joy in the presence of Christ.

He saw through a glass darkly and often grew homesick. Yet each day as he got up and prayed, he sensed again the gracious hand of God upon him. He felt no fear, only anticipation. Being with Jesus, either here or There, was Heaven.

Maureen Hay Read

Maureen Hay Read lives with her husband at Narvon, Pennsylvania. They are the parents of two daughters and two sons. Maureen presently teaches senior high students at Twin Valley Bible Academy near Morgantown, Pennsylvania.

Over the years, she has traveled extensively in the British Isles and Europe. For three years, she taught in a mission school in Beirut, Lebanon.

Her writing credits include articles in *Decision*, *Guideposts*, *Power*, *Lutheran Woman*, *Today's Christian Woman*, and *Sunday Digest*. She is also the author of two other popular books, *Like a Watered Garden* and *The Least One*.